Lean Six Sigma for Law Firms

CATHERINE ALMAN MACDONAGH

Head of legal publishing
Fiona Fleming

Publisher
Helen Donegan

Editor
Laura Slater

Published by ARK Group:

UK, Europe and Asia office
6–14 Underwood Street
London, N1 7JQ
United Kingdom
Tel: +44(0) 207 566 5792
publishing@ark-group.com

North America office
4408 N. Rockwood Drive, Suite 150
Peoria IL 61614
United States
Tel: +1 (309) 495 2853
publishingna@ark-group.com

www.ark-group.com

Layout by Susie Bell, www.f-12.co.uk

Printed by Canon (UK) Ltd, Cockshot Hill, Reigate, RH2 8BF, United Kingdom

ISBN: 978-1-78358-111-5

A catalogue record for this book is available from the British Library

ARK Group is a division of Wilmington plc. The company is registered in England & Wales
with company number 2931372 GB
Registered office: 6-14 Underwood Street, London N1 7JQ. VAT Number: GB 899 3725 51.

Contents

Executive summary

This book is a thought leadership piece that aspires to relate the foundational concepts and vocabulary of Lean and Six Sigma and reports on how they are currently being employed in a legal context.

All law firms, wherever they may fall on the process improvement continuum, will benefit from learning about the use of Lean and Six Sigma in a legal context. Whether your firm is just beginning to hear about process improvement and project management, has started to develop skills and undertake projects, or has a fully branded initiative based on Lean Six Sigma, this book is intended to serve as a resource.

At this point, many firms have already embarked on their continuous improvement journeys. Still, many firms remain at the opposite end of the spectrum and are just "beginning to think about starting". Firms who have been waiting to find out how this is working for others will learn plenty from those who have gone before them. Some will be their direct competitors, driving them from a position of mere interest to necessity. Competitor firms may already have robust programs in place with cadres of skilled Lean and Six Sigma practitioners, a host of project managers, and dozens of completed projects backed by millions of dollars in improvement benefits.

In addition to discussions about Lean, Six Sigma, and other methodologies most helpful to those in the legal profession, this book will shine a light on firms that are already employing process improvement approaches and tools. For every firm that has launched a marketing campaign around its activities or is profiled in this book, there are dozens of firms – small, medium, and large – that are quietly and seriously developing competitive advantages via process improvement. Understandably, many firms are sensitive about the type and level of information they wish to share and make available in the marketplace. Others are using their successes as the cornerstone of their strategic plans and marketing efforts.

The point is that there is no single "right way" to do this work. The important thing is to begin to create a culture of continuous improvement in law firms. Why? Because when we do this work, we not only improve the process on which we are working, we also deliver greater value, efficiency, and predictability while increasing our quality and likelihood of successful outcomes. If that is not enough, keep this in mind: this is all done without tradeoffs; rather, it is a win-win for both the client and the firm.

I aim to accomplish several things in this book: 1) to explain what Lean and Six Sigma are; 2) to make the connection between Lean, Six Sigma, and project management; 3) to demonstrate the different ways in which Lean and Six Sigma may be employed in the legal profession; 4) to publish a preliminary collection of ideas, case studies, and legal examples for the first book of its kind on the topic of legal process improvement; and 5) to accelerate a shift toward the applicability and acceptance of process improvement in the legal profession as significantly closer to the norm. The early adopters in this space have much to teach us.

In summary, this book is for those interested in learning about the different approaches to Lean/Six Sigma, where to get started, and what the results have been for those who have already tried it.

The idea is to facilitate the adoption of process improvement strategies in law firms by defining Lean and Six Sigma and then conveying how those concepts might apply in a practical sense to the legal space. This will help firms to answer the following questions, which they should ask themselves before embarking on any process improvement program, since the discussions, considerations, and decisions will be different for each firm:

- How can we use the methodologies and toolkits of Lean and Six Sigma?
- How do we make a decision about when and where to start?
- What are our drivers for employing process improvement?
- What are the specific applications, obstacles, and lessons learned from what others have tried?
- What results have been achieved – what kinds of improvements have been made and how do they translate into benefits?
- In what ways do the framework and outcomes of process improvement help us change the conversation we have with our clients, referral sources, and prospective clients?

- How do we use process improvement to deliver greater value to the firm and our clients?
- What competitive advantages can we develop by using Lean and Six Sigma at our firm?
- How do we structure a process improvement program?
- What's next?

As Jordan Furlong wrote, "Lawyers must accept and act upon a single new reality: we cannot continue to make a living in the law the way we used to… We must create sustainable cost advantages through adoption of technologies and processes."[1] Those who do so will not just survive but thrive. Those who ignore the opportunities that exist, right now, do so at their own risk.

Reference

1. Furlong, J. "You say you want a revolution" (blog post), 20th December 2013; see www.law21.ca/2013/12/say-want-revolution.

About the author

Catherine Alman MacDonagh, JD is a Legal Lean Sigma Black Belt and a certified Six Sigma Green Belt. A former corporate counsel, Catherine is well known for her thought leadership and successes as a law firm marketing and business development professional. Now a highly rated speaker and consultant, she works with professional services firms to create competitive advantages and organizational transformation through the development, planning, and implementation of innovative strategies, process improvement projects, and business development training and coaching programs.

Catherine is an adjunct faculty at Suffolk Law School and at George Washington University (Master's in Law Firm Management). She is also the Chief Enthusiasm Officer of The Legal Mocktail, an experiential networking training program, and has her own consulting practice, FIRM Guidance. She is a co-founder of the Legal Sales and Service Organization. Catherine is co-author of two books: *The Woman Lawyer's Rainmaking Game* and *The Law Firm Associate's Guide to Personal Marketing and Selling Skills.*

Catherine is a co-founder of the Legal Sales and Service Organization (LSSO). She served on the international board, as New England Chapter President, and on many committee and task forces of the Legal Marketing Association (LMA). Honors and awards Catherine has received include: Elected Fellow, College of Law Practice Management, *Boston Business Journal*'s 40 Under 40, two years on the prestigious MLF 50 (Marketing the Law Firm Top 50) List, and several Legal Marketing Association "Your Honor" Awards.

Catherine lives in Massachusetts with husband Colin, their children, Alex and Sarah, and their two Havenese dogs, Abbie and Peaches.

Please contact Catherine at Catherine@LegalLeanSigma.com, (+001) 857 272 5695, and on Twitter @cathmacdonagh.

About the Legal Lean Sigma Institute

The Legal Lean Sigma Institute, LLC (LLSI) is the first and only organization to develop and bring to law firms and legal departments a comprehensive set of process improvement (PI) and project management (PM) certification courses, training programs, and consulting services specifically designed for the legal profession. LLSI holds a registered trademark in the term Legal Lean Sigma®.

Legal Lean Sigma Institute faculty and consultants have worked on process improvement projects and delivered courses and programs for hundreds of leaders in the legal profession, both privately and publicly, including: ACC's Value Challenge Master Class; the Association of Legal Administrators (ALA) Annual Conference; ALA's Large Law Firm Retreat; the Legal Marketing Association's Annual Conference; LSSO's RainDance Conference; the Managing Partner Forum; the College of Law Practice Management's Futures Conference; and at firm and corporate law department retreats.

History – The creation of Legal Lean Sigma®

My interest in efficiency first took root after I graduated law school and became a corporate counsel for an insolvent insurance company. After observing how paper intensive, large loss claim files were handled – and how the estate was billed more the longer the work took – I would always look at how legal work was performed and delivered from the client's perspective. My understanding and perspective widened to include the law firm's viewpoint after serving in marketing and business development roles in several firms.

After earning a Green Belt certification in Six Sigma, I knew that the concepts of controlling variation to produce greater predictability, reduce errors, and so forth applied to legal but the reality is that it took me nearly a year to bridge what I had learned in the classroom to something that was useful to my work as a director of business development in a law firm. After finally trying some things and figuring out that adding

Lean to the mix was important, I kept mentioning to my friend Wendy Duffey (in between discussions about the Boston Red Sox) that someone really ought to start teaching process improvement in the legal space.

One thing led to another and, thanks to Wendy's introduction, in 2008, I began to work with Laura J. Colcord, an expert with deep experience in process improvement in various applications and industries all over the world. Our task was to design and deliver educational programs that taught process improvement in contexts that would be immediately relevant and useful to lawyers and the business professionals who work with them.

The first Legal Lean Sigma® programs were offered under the umbrella of the Legal Sales and Service Organization (LSSO) – thanks to the interest and support of my colleagues and partners, Silvia L. Coulter and Beth Marie Cuzzone – and launched (as so many first to market ideas, services, and products are) at LSSO's RainDance Conference (also the first conference of its kind). Very quickly, the success of those endeavors, combined with the interest in consulting services, created a need for a separate business structure and, in 2010, these offerings were split out of LSSO and the Legal Lean Sigma Institute LLC was formed.

In the same year, we began teaching our two-day, Yellow Belt certification course as adjunct faculty at George Washington University's Master's in Law Firm Management program. This has offered us the opportunity to work with seasoned, accomplished professionals. Lawyers, administrators, marketers, IT, HR, and finance students both learn and teach us about the application of process improvement in various law firm settings.

In 2013, faculty were added to LLSI. In 2014, LLSI expanded the certification offerings by including another option, which was completely unique to the legal profession. LLSI's combined process improvement and project management program, was developed and is taught with Timothy B. Corcoran, a member of LLSI's adjunct faculty, 2014 president of the Legal Marketing Association, and principal of Corcoran Consulting Group.

Now, LLSI has delivered and supported projects to improve both legal and business processes, including:

- Practice-specific:
  - AA Plans;
  - E-Data/Exceptions;

- o OFCCP Audit;

- o Trademark registration; and

- o Single plaintiff discrimination/litigation.

- Business:
  - o Responses to requests for proposals and information;
  - o Events;
  - o Time keeping and billing;
  - o Lateral integration and employee on-boarding;
  - o Staffing;
  - o Document management; and
  - o Facilities management.

We have developed programs and keynotes and certified thousands of leaders in Legal Lean Sigma® (and project management) at the White, Yellow, and Green Belt levels. Our certification courses have always been approved upon application for continuing legal education credit.

Our consulting practice encompasses the full spectrum of services associated with introducing, developing, and implementing process improvement programs, including strategic planning, structuring for success and organizational development, and project support with expert facilitation and Kaizen workshops.

We are now observing an interesting new wave: privately delivered certification courses for a law firm with invited clients and client teams at each table, learning and working together for the duration of the program. We are changing the conversation through the use of PI and the way we do PI work. In so doing, we are refining the process by which law firms and clients are engaging in relationships and cultivating cultures of continuous improvement.

Acknowledgements

Out of all of the things I've done professionally, process improvement in the legal profession is the most creative, fun, and challenging. It changes the conversation from "us/them" to just "us". It provides the framework and tools that allow us to translate vision into strategy, and strategy into tactics in ways that are competitive, yet allow everyone to win. It's the most rewarding work I have ever done. It is not something one does alone, however, so I am indebted to many who make it possible for me to teach and work in this space.

Thank you to all of my clients: those who have embraced the work and mission of the Legal Lean Sigma Institute, all the Green, Yellow, and White Belts certified in Legal Lean Sigma®, I appreciate you giving us the opportunity to work with you and to improve the legal profession, one process at a time. Teaching people about Lean Sigma and working on projects has enabled me to work with some of brightest people I have ever met and be part of high functioning and excellent teams – it is an honor. Each client and program participant has helped us to continuously improve our courses and consulting practice with feedback and suggestions.

Thank you, Carl A. Leonard and Dr. Stephen Chitwood, for your early and ongoing support. It is an enormous privilege to teach Legal Lean Sigma® in George Washington University's Master's in Law Firm Management Program and I thank you for the opportunities to work with you. Thank you to each and every impressive student for allowing me to learn from you in the process of teaching.

Thank you to Suffolk University Law School for the chance to teach the first combined process improvement and project management course in a law school, especially Andrew Perlman (director, Institute on Law Practice Technology and Innovation, director, Legal Technology and Innovation Concentration, professor of Law) and Ilene Seidman (associate dean for Academic Affairs and clinical professor of Law). You are pioneers and I thank you for allowing me to take part in the transformation of legal education with you. A very special thank you to the Suffolk Law students who became the first law school class in the world to be certified Legal Lean Sigma Yellow Belts in the spring 2014 semester.

Most importantly, as always, I thank my family, friends, and colleagues for their love and support with special appreciation to Colin for holding down the fort while I travel for work. You have been the reason I have been able to pursue and realize my entrepreneurial dreams, including launching the Legal Lean Sigma Institute. To my children, Sarah and Alex, the lights of my life, thank you for your sacrifices; it isn't easy to have a Mom who travels so much. I'm grateful to have the good fortune of showing you that when you are able to do something you truly enjoy, it doesn't seem so much like work. My wish is that you both find that thing that brings you the same, immense personal and professional satisfaction and sense of fulfillment.

Cheers to all who are working to improve processes in the legal profession around the world; I hope to learn about the results of your efforts and wish you great success.

Catherine Alman MacDonagh, JD

Foreword

In 1999, under the leadership of CEO and chairman Chad Holliday, DuPont embarked upon its Six Sigma journey, which was designed to eliminate costs, drive efficiency, and accelerate the company's transformation. It was clearly understood by all corporate officers in attendance at this kick-off that no business, staff function, or region was exempt. This was a business imperative – one that could arguably determine the company's future. While our initial focus was upon cost reduction, the power of Six Sigma was, as we subsequently learned, more than that. Shortly thereafter, I was tapped to assume the role of Six Sigma champion for Legal.

While Six Sigma was initially met with skepticism in some quarters, Legal leadership had gained considerable credibility over the previous eight years in leading a law firm and supplier convergence process and in the implementation of the DuPont Legal Model, which emphasized the importance of applying business discipline and data in our representation of DuPont. In short, we were able to recognize early on that process improvement matters and that, if it was embraced by Legal, it could provide us with a means to contribute to the company's transformation. So, we began to implement function-wide Six Sigma with no practice group, profession, or region exempted.

As an aside, several years into the initiative at a subsequent corporate officers meeting, our outside speaker, Jeff Immelt, who was among two others vying to succeed Jack Welch as CEO of General Electric, spoke to the group about the power of Six Sigma. At this point, GE was "all in" and was driving this initiative throughout the corporation with typical Jack Welch intensity. Mr Immelt spoke with great persuasion and intensity about the impact of Six Sigma upon GE. And as if that wasn't compelling enough, he stated to the officers in attendance, "And even the lawyers can do it!" That was all that I needed as further provocation. From that point forward, we drove process improvement at all levels of the organization and with our network of providers with great resolve.

The impact upon our culture through the implementation of Six Sigma has been incredibly forceful and telling. Under the broad heading of process improvement, our professionals have developed and honed their leadership, communication, and collaboration skills – and, most significantly, their bottom-line focus. The program has evolved to embrace certainly Six Sigma, Lean Six Sigma, and project management – all of which serve to drive process improvement. Collectively, these tools have served to enable Legal to speak the language of the business, drive efficiency, and deliver superior results by any metric or criterion one might choose.

So I applaud Catherine in creating this primer on process improvement. It is critically needed by our profession, which suffers all too often from the perception that lawyers, and perhaps others that labor in this field, are above it all, and that business discipline and process add little value, and may even undermine our creativity and professionalism. So, let me close by observing that the examples shared in this publication of lawyers applying process improvement methodologies and tools are very compelling and serve as testament to Mr Immelt's observation that "Even the lawyers can do it". Yes, they can!!

Thomas L. Sager, senior vice president and general counsel, DuPont Legal

Introduction: Diagnosing and overcoming lawyers' resistance to process improvement

By Jordan Furlong, author, consultant, and legal industry analyst

Many lawyers show ongoing reluctance, in the face of overwhelming market pressures, to fully adopt the principles and practices of business process improvement.

Consider the following elements of the global legal market in 2014.

- All but the most elite large and midsize law firms in the US, the UK, and Canada are bleeding: revenue is down; realization is nearing 80 percent; profits have fallen; clients are driving change; and partners are angry or scared. The cutting, and the firing, and the free-agent lateral hiring has all been done; there is nothing left now but recognition and acceptance that the traditional law firm business structure is no longer competitive in this market.

  Lawyer control of the legal market is fading fast: In England and Wales, more than 300 alternative business structures, owned wholly or in part by people who are not lawyers, now provide legal services; three US states have either licensed "non-lawyers" to provide basic services or are figuring out how to do so; independent paralegals are licensed by law societies (or on the way there) in four Canadian provinces, with ABSs not far behind.

- Legal technology and process companies are in ascendance: Neota Logic has partnered with two AmLaw 100 law firms; United Lex has taken over the litigation support functions of a third; LegalZoom is working with ODR pioneer Modria. Novus Law is taking untold dollars away from law firms. Apps can draft contracts and answer legal questions. Predictive coding is taking discovery work away from litigators. And on and on.

- New ways to organize legal talent and sell its services are flourishing: Four major British law firms (Berwin Leighton Paisner, Eversheds, Pinsent Masons, and Allen & Overy) have set up affiliated project lawyer agencies; Axiom Law is taking on complete deal work; Keystone Law is expanding to Australia; Quality Solicitors is offering a completely new business model to consumer law providers (at fixed prices, no less); LegalZoom has soft-launched in the UK in conjunction with Quality Solicitors, neck-and-neck with Rocket Lawyer.

And yet I still see people in this industry asking, "Where's the revolution? When is the change going to come?" Folks, *the change is here*. We're living it. Cast your mind back about five years – when Richard Susskind had just published *The End of Lawyers?* – and ask yourself whether you thought this much upheaval, and advancement, and innovation was possible in such a short period. Cast it back 10 years, when the "blawgosphere" barely existed, and ask the same. The legal market is becoming more diverse and more accessible every year; legal services are more affordable and more predictably priced every year.

Most importantly, the pace of that change is accelerating. Alternatives to the traditional – in terms of service providers, business models, workflow systems, delivery vehicles, pricing strategies, and so on – are becoming normalized; that is, they're spoken of less frequently as "alternative" and more frequently as simply another option. We don't even talk about the "new normal" as much – it's all becoming normal. These are not the signs of change in retreat; these are the signs of change becoming mainstream – ceasing to be "change" and starting to become "the way things are".

The problem is that everyone seems to have received the memo about change in the legal market – except the legal profession itself. Too many lawyers still place their hands firmly over their ears when these conversations begin – or, if they do listen, they immediately come up with all sorts of reasons why their own corner of the legal world will stay the same, or why they could not possibly undertake any of the necessary responses without destroying their businesses or abandoning their professional duties. These are the rationalizations of people who resist change primarily on the grounds that they just do not want to do it.

An excellent example can be found in lawyers' ongoing reluctance to truly embrace business process improvement within their firms. For a profession suffering from aggravated clients, shrinking revenues, competitive inertia, archaic business practices, and system waste, process improvement is the nearest we will come to meeting the definition of "panacea". It is easy to understand, inexpensive to implement, lowers costs, improves quality, enhances communication, facilitates lawyer training, makes fixed fees profitable, and makes clients happy. If it could cure disease and direct an Oscar-winning movie, it could hardly be a more attractive proposition.

And yet, with few (albeit happily increasing) exceptions, there is still not much enthusiasm for it among lawyers and law firms. There is an odd reluctance to embrace something that clearly delivers so many benefits. Identifying the source of that reluctance tells us something important about lawyers and our capacity to adapt to this new legal marketplace.

"It's pretty tough to get lawyers to change their ways", said one partner at a big firm that is starting to implement legal project management. Another partner approached LPM training with a familiar apprehension: "Doesn't this apply only to commodity practices?" Resistance to innovation fits lawyers to a T. But what really comes across from these accounts is a sense that lawyers are not trying process improvement or workflow management primarily because they do not want to do so.

This resistance does not, I think, have much to do with lawyers' inability to grasp process improvement's features or benefits. I think it has much more to do with lawyers' dislike of procedure, systematization, methodology, routine – with "process", a word many lawyers still use with a certain amount of distaste.

I think that is because we lawyers pride ourselves on our capacity for ingenuity: the unexpected insight that makes a deal possible, the brilliant argument that turns a trial around, the stroke of inspiration that not only saves the day but also shows off just how bright we are. Smart people are drawn to the law like moths to a flame, and one of the things about smart people is that we prize raw intelligence over plodding procedure. We use loaded adjectives – "drudge", "mindless", "humdrum", "grunt" (and several less polite words) – to describe legal work that requires limited imagination, consistency over brilliance, and a lot of attention to detail.

Now, any real reflection on the matter will show that work of this nature is no less valuable or worthy than the racier, hyper-intelligent work most lawyers crave – but in our professional culture, there is a clear distinction between the two, and it matters. (In this same vein, note the tone in which lawyers say the word "commoditization".)

It is a distinction, unfortunately, that we draw at our peril. Our competitors, some inside the legal profession but most of them outside it, have no qualms about embracing workflow improvement and the systems-based benefits it confers. They look at the way lawyers have traditionally gone about our work, and they see countless inefficiencies just asking to be exploited.

Whenever a legal task is subjected to a flowchart, outsourced to a lower-cost resource, or converted to a software algorithm, process improvement is at work, exposing all the ways in which traditional lawyering not only wastes time and money but also fails to deliver the most effective and accurate result. We give document review and due diligence tasks to bright young associates with zero training and zero interest in the job; our competitors apply rigorous scanning, screening, and review templates by trained workers who actually like to do this sort of thing. Who do you suppose gets better results?

The day of the haphazard lawyer, who pursues solutions by intuition, experience, and the loosest possible timetable, is drawing to a close. In their place is emerging the process-driven lawyer: disciplined, procedural, and systematic, who understands that madness lies not in method, but in its absence.

Most lawyers do not like that idea. We would much prefer to maintain the image of the ingenious lawyer who triumphs by intellect rather than by procedural discipline. It confirms our belief in our innate intellectual advantage over non-lawyer competitors – and, frankly, it makes us feel better about ourselves. At some level, we take offense at the idea of process improvement because it seems to reduce this wonderful profession of ours to little more than a series of steps, a collection of decision trees that anyone could follow.

The truth is, much of what lawyers do can in fact be charted, diagrammed, and proceduralized, and both the quality and the cost will be better for it. But that does not mean there is no room for smart, creative lawyers in the future.

For one thing, systems do not need to be straightforward and monotonous. More often than not, especially in the law, they are complex and challenging, and they can easily be made elegant, precise, finely tuned, honed to a keen edge – the imagery of swordsmanship is intentional. Even within systems, a lawyer's unique judgment, analysis, and creativity can emerge.

Legal service providers who adopt systematic workflow processes will be more successful than those who do not; there is no doubt in my mind about this. So like it or not, we will have to embrace this new methodology. But what I really want to urge lawyers to do is, in fact, to like it.

Process is not a diminution of our intellectual gifts; it is the honing, disciplining, and improvement of them. Frameworks and road maps have never hurt anyone; they have gotten things built and changed lives far more effectively and comfortably than we could have managed in their absence. Take a new approach to process – look at it with a fresh eye, and see what it can add to your professional life rather than what it can take away. Process does not have to be a necessary evil. It can easily be a necessary good.

Jordan Furlong is an author, consultant, and legal industry analyst who tracks the rapidly changing legal services environment and advises law firms and legal organizations how best to respond. He writes about the new legal market at the award-winning blog Law21.ca, from which parts of this article were adapted. Furlong's blog, Law21: Dispatches from a Legal Profession on the Brink, *has been named one of the 100 best law blogs in North America for six straight years by the* ABA Journal.

Chapter 1:
An introduction to Lean and Six Sigma

What is process improvement?

Let's start with the basics. What, exactly, is "process improvement"? A primary goal of this book is to provide an introduction to the two most important process improvement toolkits (Lean and Six Sigma) for law firms, the main concepts behind each, and the jargon used by Legal Lean Sigma®.

Most people can identify when there are "issues" with a process. Far fewer can thoughtfully respond to the questions:

- How would you decide which problems are the most important to solve?

- How will you know when you have succeeded in improving a process?

Process improvement (sometimes called legal process improvement or LPI) provides a framework and tools to answer these two critical questions.

This book contains an overview of process improvement, process measurement, the five key phases (define, measure, analyze, improve, control) in executing a process improvement project, and the major steps and most common tools used in each phase of a process improvement project. In discussing what is required to move beyond carrying out process improvements opportunistically, I hope not only to make the case for starting a program and eventually carrying out process improvement systematically, but to help the reader to make the case as well.

To begin, then, it is helpful to define what we mean by "process improvement". It is the systematic practice of first analyzing a process to understand how it is *currently* carried out, then searching for issues, problems, and opportunities in the process and prioritizing them. Once prioritized, tools and techniques are employed to solve priority problems or to capture significant opportunities. Finally, the new process must be controlled so that it delivers the anticipated benefits.

A "process" is a describable, repeatable sequence of activities that generates an outcome; as such, to a process improvement practitioner, nearly everything qualifies as a process, from the mundane routines of everyday life (like making coffee or tea) to incredibly complex processes involving multiple operations, people, organizations, and so forth (such as class action law suits). In the words of W. Edwards Deming, who was known as the Father of the Quality Revolution, and was responsible for the first application of statistical quality control principles to a non-manufacturing environment, "If you can't describe what you are doing as a process, you don't know what you are doing."

Already, based on my experience, I anticipate that there are readers who are unconvinced (and may be bristling with the notion) that the legal work they do can be considered or distilled to "a process". One of the things I often hear from clients is that "we don't have a process for that". However, the reality is that if you are doing a particular kind of work right now, you have a process – albeit one that may radically differ from matter to matter, client to client, lawyer to lawyer, or office to office. Moreover, we consider processes to be the way that law firms create and deliver value to their clients. Thus, we recognize that processes embody the knowledge of the law firm, department, practice group, or team. In short, our processes are the way we do and deliver our work. Ideally, they are the best way we have learned or know how to do something – they are our best practices. As such, a great process can create a competitive advantage for a law firm.

What is legal project management?
There is a direct connection between process improvement and project management (also called legal project management or LPM). Consider this: what is the benefit of having the ability to manage projects very well if our underlying process is not the best it can be? Conversely, what is the value of having an excellent process that is not being managed well?

Process improvement helps us determine the best way to carry out a certain kind of work to achieve efficiency, excellent quality of work and service, high probability of successful outcomes, and predictability. When we do develop the capacity to do process improvement work, we can employ project management skills to select the best processes, tools, and skills to be able to carry out our ideal process every time.

Essentially, project management is a role and set of skills that ensure that, for a particular engagement, we review and select the right processes and then apply them appropriately to each particular matter. Then, project management involves actively managing schedules, staff, and deliverables to deliver high quality work on time and under budget to achieve specific goals.

Timothy B. Corcoran, principal of the Corcoran Consulting Group and adjunct faculty and affiliated consultant of the Legal Lean Sigma Institute, defines project management as "the process and activity of planning, organizing, motivating, and controlling resources, procedures and protocols". So, even project management may be considered a process.

Corcoran explains the six steps of project management as follows:

1. Define objective (what constitutes a win for the client?).

2. Define scope and constraints, e.g. budget, timeline.

3. Establish the project plan. (Identify standard, variable, and volatile tasks; establish task timelines and budgets. What is on the "critical path"? What resources are necessary, *including a project manager*?)

4. Execute the plan (track efforts, time, budget, results).

5. Continuously monitor performance, change management (including regular communication and establishing a continuous "feedback loop").

6. Review and improve. (Learning organizations focus on improvement over time.)

Where to start?

Many firms ask: "in which discipline should we invest and engage first, process improvement or project management?" The simple answer is that there is no one "right way" to begin. That stated, my bias is for firms to learn both at once; this is why the Legal Lean Sigma Institute developed the only certification courses that combine Lean, Six Sigma, and project management. My next best suggestion is to engage in process improvement first, so that a firm begins to improve processes and simultaneously to develop project management skills. After that, the firm can train project managers and others using optimized processes.

Whether your firm begins with process improvement or project management, eventually, both must be employed for the firm to fully realize the benefits of either one. We are able to attain a multiplier effect when we combine process improvement and project management: we have better, more standardized processes that are well controlled in order to achieve a high level of performance.

Processes always exist to serve a client. Accordingly, we measure both the process performance and efficiency. Processes have a characteristic performance level, usually called process capability, that describes how well the process meets client expectations (which means, obviously, that we need to understand the client's expectations as well). Additionally, we learn about process resource requirements, sometimes called process efficiency, which refers to the resources (time, people, equipment, money) required to carry out the process. There are many dimensions along which a process may be measured. Moreover, a process may perform quite well in some dimensions and poorly in others.

Ronald L. Burdge points out the value of measuring client satisfaction: "The legal profession frequently proclaims it is dedicated to providing legal services in a way that satisfies... But if we do not measure the quality of that service, then can we really say that we are able to provide excellent legal representation? If you don't know that you are doing good work, can you really be sure you are? If what you value is a satisfied client, then you must determine how to satisfy a client – and you will not really be able to know that until you understand how to gauge client satisfaction in the first place."

What are Lean and Six Sigma?

Now that we have process basics covered, we can delve into Lean and Six Sigma. Lean is about simplifying processes. With Lean, we simplify processes, reduce the number of steps, maximize process speed, and greatly improve productivity – we focus on doing the right things and eliminating waste in processes. In this way, we ensure that we maximize resource efficiency. Six Sigma is focused on reducing and controlling variation. Put together, Lean Sigma is about deciding the best way to do something and then always doing those things correctly.

In short, the two disciplines are about establishing the right things to do (Lean) and then doing those things right (Six Sigma). While it used to be the case that practitioners of each might have argued that their way was better, now they are considered complementary and used together. Some use the term Lean Six Sigma, others use Lean Sigma, which is actually an example of Lean in action, since it eliminates "six" as a superfluous word. That said, both terms are correct and are used interchangeably.

Lean concepts have been applied for centuries, but a major development in this line of thinking occurred in the Japanese automobile industry in the middle of the 20th century:

> "As Kiichiro Toyoda, Taiichi Ohno, and others at Toyota looked at this situation [of the automobile manufacturing process] in the 1930s, and more intensely just after World War II, it occurred to them that a series of simple innovations might make it more possible to provide both continuity in process flow and a wide variety in product offerings... and [they] invented the Toyota Production System.
>
> This system in essence shifted the focus of the manufacturing engineer from individual machines and their utilization, to the flow of the product through the total process. Toyota concluded that by right-sizing machines for the actual volume needed, introducing self-monitoring machines to ensure quality, lining the machines up in process sequence, pioneering quick setups so each machine could make small volumes of many part numbers, and having each process step notify the previous step of its current needs for materials, it would be possible to obtain low cost, high variety, high quality, and very rapid throughput times to respond to changing customer desires. Also, information management could be made much simpler and more accurate."[1]

How do we translate process improvement to a legal context?

One of our challenges is to translate the concepts of process improvement so that they make sense in a legal context. After all, law firms are not manufacturing automobiles or silicon wafers. There is a great deal of variation: each firm, practice group, lawyer, client, jurisdiction, matter, case, set of facts, judge, opposing counsel, and so on, is different. So how can we ensure that the desire to eliminate something in a process does not replace the exercise of good judgment or constrain our ability to do something that is in the best interests of the firm and its client?

This translation of these concepts from the manufacturing world to the legal space is why Legal Lean Sigma® was created. The use of Lean and Six Sigma in law is simple on a conceptual level but not always easy in the application. We have found that it has always been easiest for candidates in our certification courses to understand how to use process improvement in relation to business processes such as timekeeping, client intake, or conflicts. Initially, it can be more of a stretch to think about how these concepts might be applied to legal work since there can often be quite a bit of variation in terms of how lawyers like to do and deliver particular kinds of work.

However, if we consider that every service offered, whether it is litigation or transactional work, contains a series of repeatable, describable steps – even if there is variation in each one – then each one is a process. Accordingly, in each service offering, there are abundant opportunities to apply Lean concepts and tools to make the process simpler and faster.

The application of Lean concepts to a service company

In an October 2003 Harvard Business Review *article entitled "The Lean Service Machine", Cynthia Karen Swank related how a service company was able to apply lessons learned from manufacturing. The article is particularly relevant, considering that many large law firms have grown through mergers, acquisitions, and combinations. Moreover, most firms have identified service as a key strategy for differentiation, just like Jefferson Pilot Financial, as Swank describes:*

"Jefferson Pilot Financial was typical of many U.S. service companies at the end of the 1990s. After making four acquisitions that more than tripled its size, the full-service life insurance and annuities company was searching for new ways to grow in a fiercely competitive business environment. Rising customer expectations had led to a proliferation of new insurance products as well as an increase in product complexity and costs. At the same time, specialized niche players touting lower premiums and faster handling of policies were forcing full-service insurance providers to both improve service and reduce costs.

The top managers of Jefferson Pilot Financial (JPF) recognized that the company needed to differentiate itself in the eyes of its customers, the independent life-insurance advisers who sell and service policies... It identified superior service to them as a key ingredient of that strategy.

To determine where improved service would have the greatest impact, JPF undertook an in-depth analysis of the operations... The study unearthed considerable variation in the quality of existing services... It was clear that management could significantly increase revenue by improving operations. Indeed, the company estimated that it could increase the paid annualized premium for its Premier Partners by 10% to 15% if it could issue all policies within three weeks of receiving the applications, offer periodic application status reports, simplify the submission process, and reduce errors to 1%.

JPF believed that its business could benefit from lean production because its operations involved the processing of an almost tangible 'service product.' Like an automobile on the assembly line, an insurance policy goes through a series of processes, from initial application to underwriting, or risk assessment, to policy issuance. With each step, value is added to the work in progress – just as a car gets doors or a coat of paint.

In late 2000, on the advice of a consulting firm, JPF appointed a five-person 'lean team' to reengineer the New Business operations according to the principles of lean production. The team included the assistant vice president of New Business administration and a special project manager who reported directly to the senior vice president overseeing New Business operations. They were supported by three lean-production experts from the consulting firm. Thus the team combined in-depth knowledge of JPF's processes with an understanding of lean-production principles.

The initiative has delivered impressive results. The company halved the average time from receipt of a Premier Partner application to issuance of a policy, reduced labor costs by 26%, and trimmed the rate of reissues due to errors by 40%... These outcomes contributed to a remarkable 60% increase in new annualized life premiums in the company's core individual-life-insurance business in just two years. Similar results are being recorded in other departments as the company rolls out the new systems across the whole organization."

If we replace key terms in this case with legal examples, the applicability of Lean to law firms becomes more obvious: Law Firm A was typical of many similarly situated firms. After making four acquisitions that more than tripled its size, the full-service law firm was searching for new ways to grow in a fiercely competitive business environment. Rising client expectations had led to a proliferation of service offerings as well as an increase in service delivery complexity and costs. At the same time, specialized niche players touting lower premiums and faster handling of legal services, such as document review, were forcing full-service law firms to both improve service and reduce costs.

The executive committee of Law Firm A recognized that the firm needed to differentiate itself in the eyes of its clients, prospects, and referral sources. Law Firm A identified superior service to them as a key ingredient of that strategy.

It was clear that the firm could significantly increase revenue by improving operations. Indeed, the firm estimated that it could increase the profits per partner by 10–15 percent if it could speed up the delivery of legal work to the most utilized services of its key clients within three weeks of receiving the request for work, offer periodic status and budget reports, simplify the intake process, and reduce errors to 1 percent.

Using Lean thinking to eliminate waste

Lean thinking relentlessly searches for and then reduces and even eliminates eight kinds of waste:

1. Defects and all related waste, including inspection, testing, and correction: Examples of defects include missing a filing deadline, incomplete forms, bad drafting, data entry errors, and omissions;

2. Overproduction: Examples include starting work before clearing conflicts, printing too many hard copies, and drafting a 10-page memo when only a one-page summary was requested;

3. Waiting: Examples include awaiting responses from clients, employees, or opposing counsel, starting a call or meeting late due to late arrivals, waiting for technology such as boot up/restart times;

4. Excess capacity: For example, not using the lowest cost resources such as clients, paralegals, and assistants that are capable of doing tasks, when partners are doing associate-level work, or over-staffing a matter;

5. Transportation (this type of waste refers to things moving as opposed to people moving, which is considered "motion"): Examples include moving files from one place to another and sending hardcopies rather than emails;

6. Inventory: Examples include work in process (WIP), unread email, marketing materials (such as collateral, brochures, and promotional items, or event materials);

7. Motion (which refers to people moving as opposed to things): Examples include people spending extra time getting from one place to the next due to travel or poor office layout, delivering files rather than mailing/emailing them, extra keystrokes/clicks to find documents; and

8. Extra processing steps: Examples include conducting too much research or double and triple checking (e.g. approvals of expenses without any real review).

Waste is present in virtually every process. In their Lean management guide, "Lean for Legal Staff – The 7 Hidden Wastes", legal services consultants and trainers Levantar give examples of how work in progress (WIP) is created through waste: "One department found that 40% of in the inputs (paperwork and forms) it received from clients contained errors or omissions. To correct these, the legal staff had to call the clients; we know from our work in call centres that only 1 in 3 outbound calls is successful… Imagine therefore that for every 100 matters being processed there were 180 activities generated."[2]

Using Six Sigma to reduce variation

Lean is better when we add Six Sigma, which is focused on reducing process variation to reduce errors and defects. Our concentration is on understanding relationships between many variables. Those include the relationships between inputs and outputs, the key factors that affect outcomes, and the "best way" to do something (i.e. how can we increase our probability of a positive outcome). We question how carefully a process needs to be controlled in order to give the results desired by the client, and ask what are the benefits of consistency and standardization?

While Lean is focused on resource efficiency, with Six Sigma, our focus is on process capability and alignment with requirements. Process capability is what your process can deliver. Therefore, with Six Sigma, we want a capable process that is aligned with requirements. When we reduce and control variation so that we are doing things right, we create a very capable process.

A Six Sigma process is one where there are only 3.4 defects per million opportunities (DPMO). We define "opportunity" as any chance not to meet the required specifications. This standard makes perfect sense in the context of a manufacturing environment where Six Sigma was originally developed (first at Motorola, in the early 1980s, and later at other companies such as AlliedSignal, Boeing, or General Electric, where it was famously championed by the former CEO, Jack Welch).

Sigma	Defects per million opportunities
1	691,462
2	308,538
3	66,807
4	6,210
5	233
6	3.4

Figure 1: DPMO in Six Sigma processes

The art and science of legal process improvement

At its core, Six Sigma revolves around a few key concepts. The first is "critical to quality", which are the attributes that are most important to the client(s). A "defect" is any failure to deliver what the client wants. We must always keep in mind that variation is what our clients experience, what they see and feel; clients want to be pleased, not surprised, so it is important to have "stable operations" which ensure that we have consistent, predictable processes to improve what the client sees and feels.

NovusLaw offers document review, management, and analysis for lawyers. They offer a stunning case study on the applicability of Six Sigma to the document review process and also serve as an example of an industry driver and innovator: "Six Sigma is what we use to eliminate defects as we measure and analyze our work processes. Typically, undocumented processes will yield 20,000–60,000 defects per million opportunities. Six Sigma is designed to get that down to fewer than 4/ million. On our most recent document review we performed at Five Sigma, or approximately 200 defects per million. By the way, that's about 200 times better than the average in the legal industry today."[3]

This type of work used to be routinely performed by law firms. Now, law firms may do very well to partner with an outsourced provider who can deliver greater predictability and much higher quality work at a predictable price.

Not every step or part of every process should be standardized or controlled as tightly as another step in the same process – this is why legal process improvement is both art and science. There may be plenty of steps that require us to allow for a lot of latitude as we need to build in room for variation based on the lawyer's experience and knowledge. Other steps require little to no judgment and are therefore good candidates for controlling variation. Every case or matter does not need to be approached as though we had never done this kind of work before; this is not efficient and it also actively contradicts what we say to our clients, prospects, and referral sources about the benefits of working with lawyers who have great experience.

The foundation of process improvement is to describe (map) the process. Then, we measure the process. Each process has a characteristic performance level and characteristic resource requirements. The process performance (also called process capability) describes how well the process meets client expectations, while the process resource requirements (also called process efficiency) refers to the resources (time, people, equipment, and costs) required to carry out the process. There are many dimensions along which a process can be measured; a process can perform well in some dimensions and poorly in others.

Lean is used to understand process efficiency and Six Sigma helps us to understand process capability and align the process with requirements. Thus, we now use Lean Sigma (or Lean Six Sigma) for they are complementary and, used together, offer the most relevant and effective approach to employing process improvement in the legal industry. There is no question that opportunities for improvements in law firms are everywhere. When we employ the thinking of Lean Sigma we cannot help but see many chances to make things better in our processes for both the client and our firm – *with no tradeoffs*.

There are some who find it difficult to see the process behind the art of doing and delivering legal work. However, whatever kind of work a lawyer or firm is currently doing, it most certainly involves a process – it may not be a good one, but there are steps that are being followed each time. Since lawyers and law firms the world over seem to be far more easily persuaded by precedent than by the idea of being the first to innovate, this book contains compelling case studies as to how Lean and Six Sigma have been applied in the legal profession.

Five principles of process improvement

Lean Sigma is both a methodology and a toolkit. The methodology consists of investigating a process and improving it by using a set of five principles in a particular sequence:

1. Specify value in the eyes of the client: We use the client's perspective to evaluate whether an activity is value-adding (activities that work to create a feature or attribute the client is willing to pay for) or non-value-adding (activities that take time and resources, but do not create additional value for the client). All non-value-adding activities are priority candidates for elimination or minimization.

2. Reduce waste and variation: In addition to minimizing or eliminating the eight kinds of waste, we are also cognizant of the fact that processes are harder to operate and require more resources if they vary. Also, when processes vary, sometimes the results will be outside the client's acceptable range.

3. Make value flow at the pull of the client: When a process has "flow", the steps are linked together so that we move from one value-adding activity directly to another, without stopping or waiting. Non-value-adding steps have been eliminated and activities are now very close together. This means that there is no waiting or batching and the process takes the shortest possible time from the beginning to the end. This short cycle time allows a law firm to be very responsive to the client. The idea of "pull" is that a law firm is able to create value directly in response to actual client demand. Providing exactly what the client wants and acting exactly when the client wants (and at the last possible moment) requires all process steps to be closely coordinated in order to work together seamlessly.

4. Align and empower employees: To successfully and continuously improve processes, the firm must harness the power of great teams. There are teams of grouped individuals, where each member of the team is carrying out separate aspects of a project. There are also teams that act as an extension of the leader. The integrated, true team is able to leverage individual strengths to achieve extraordinary capacity for coordinated action – this is the kind of team we are aiming for not only when we deliver process improvement projects but in the teams delivering client work and service.

5. Continuously improve in pursuit of perfection: Because changes in the business environment are constant and rapid, they create requirements for higher process capabilities and efficiencies. If we do not continuously improve, we lose our ability to compete and function.

Maintaining the client's perspective

Notice that we begin our inquiry into Lean Sigma by using the client's perspective to evaluate whether any activity is value-adding (activities that work to create a feature or attribute the client is willing to pay for) or non-value-adding (activities that take time and resources, but do not create additional value for the client). Non-value-added activities are priority candidates for elimination or minimization. Of course, we do not just indiscriminately cut anything or anyone from a process. In fact, there are many occasions where we actually need more people/resources to make a process efficient. Moreover, just because value is not clear to the client, that does not necessary mean that the step should be eliminated; it is an opportunity to have a discussion about why something is necessary, advisable, or important to do from the lawyer's perspective. Even after discussion, the client might not find the activity valuable – this is an even greater reason to be highly efficient.

For any of your processes, consider:

- What is the value of the process in the eyes of the client?
- How do you establish this (or how would you find out)?
- What do you do that your clients might not consider valuable?
- What waste is there in the process?
- What are the effects of variation in your processes on your firm and on your clients?

Lean Sigma is the methodology and toolkit that provides a way to explore and answer these key questions.

References

1. Lean Enterprise Institute; see www.lean.org/WhatsLean/History.cfm.
2. First published in March 2012 and most recently updated in February 2013; see www.levantar.co.uk/index.php/lean-consulting-training-strategy-reviews/lean-management-process-improvement-free-lean-guide-to.
3. Adam Smith, Esq. LLC, "Conversation with Ray Bayley of NovusLaw"; see www.adamsmithesq.com/2008/06/a_conversation_with_ray_b.

Chapter 2:
The case for process improvement

Most processes fall far short of their potential

What Lean Sigma practitioners often find is that the processes people think are in place do not really exist. Or we find that each person has his or her own process. Or that the processes take much longer than people believe. As Henry Ford famously said, "Most people spend more time and energy going around problems than in trying to solve them." What we see in law firms is that most people are spending more time and energy in solving problems created by ineffective processes than in trying to improve them.

In many cases, we have seen that what started out as a fairly decent practice has changed considerably over the years. Usually, this is due to well-intentioned workers who employ "workarounds" in order to compensate for the failure of the process to support the person working with it. The result is that law firm processes often, by lack of attention or intention, wind up looking like New England farmhouses: built in a random fashion; tacking on one thing after another as the years pass by; and producing a result that looks nothing like what one would have designed if the architect had started to draft the plans with the current requirements in mind.

Those who have employed Lean and/or Six Sigma will attest to the fact that, as soon as we start to describe and measure a process, we will begin to see things that could be improved, either in the client's eyes or the eyes of the firm/department – or both.

In fact, most of our processes fall far short of their potential and improving them will benefit *both* the client and the firm/department. The reality is that if we continue to operate our processes as we always have while expectations of clients, owners, regulators, etc. rise, we will inevitably experience a performance gap. However, if we improve our processes before those expectations rise, we will develop significant advantages.

Understanding changing client expectations

The other thing we will do when we begin to learn about and engage in process improvement is demonstrate our ability to speak our client's language. As Karen Dalton and John Dugga observe, "While lawyers generally know their clients well, they are often surprised at how much their clients know about Lean, Six Sigma, project management, and even agile. Clients expect exceptional legal expertise, but what they are most interested in is how the firm is going to do their work. Clients are very interested and receptive to innovative value-added services that deliver results."[1]

DuPont believes that legal professionals should bear some responsibility for their client's bottom-line success and that legal services, no less than other services, can improve through process analysis. They say process improvement is for lawyers who "are driven by a commitment to continuous improvement and who recognize that the complete lawyer brings more to the table than legal acumen".[2]

As, to be cost-effective, work must be done by the lowest cost resource that is capable of performing it, process improvement and project management becomes critical. Detailed knowledge of the effort required to carry out the work is required, recording time very important, analyzing past engagements is key, according to David Hargis, chief operating officer at Tucker Ellis & West, who suggests that "metrics shift from the billable hour, and that new capabilities are required – profitability methodology, reward systems".

With that in mind, it would be difficult to reasonably argue the point that process efficiency and ongoing improvement in any professional services work is a bad thing. Yet for years the legal profession has managed business in a manner that creates disincentives to do so. The billable hour is one such distinguishing riptide. Thompson Hine is an example of one firm that has established a clear and structured path to keep the focus on delivering what the client wants in the way the client wants it, rather than anchoring on historic ways of undertaking client work.

"Our clients tell us regularly, through our formal surveys, our client summit and ongoing discussions that great work is more than just understanding the legal discipline. It is as much about how that work is delivered. Great work demands excellence in how it is outlined, staffed, monitored, and managed, with diligent communication from beginning to post-close. General industry has understood this philosophy for years. We have the benefit of that roadmap to apply within our firm – and we have invested the time and resources to get it right," says Sue Brelus, chief marketing officer at Thompson Hine.

Thompson Hine's director of legal project management, Bill Garcia, notes examples where the rigor of comprehensive legal project management has enabled the firm to increase efficiency and meet very short timelines under tight budget constraints: "Client needs vary based on the matter. This process forces the upfront discussion that puts a clear spotlight on what is valued most in the particular situation. Agreement on what defines success, followed by carefully outlined process, monitoring the process, reporting to identify issues, and continuous communication empower firms to optimize service delivery. Without all the pieces, process may be improved, but it will not be optimized", remarks Garcia. "The LPM conversation between client and outside counsel forces self-examination, which leads to improvement."

Convincing lawyers to embrace Lean Sigma and project management is no small undertaking. In fact, both the change management and the work of process improvement itself require vision, commitment, serious discipline, and proper allocation of resources. However, we must accept the fact that most lawyers, either by training or nature (or both) seem to approach even the notion of change with a large dose of skepticism. We seem to challenge everything and base our thinking and decisions on precedent, rather than the possibilities and benefits that innovation may deliver to them.

Moreover, many lawyers initially resist the notion that their work can be reduced to a series of steps where predictability of activity and budgets are possible. It is important to recognize that their concerns have some merit. Lean Sigma will not work for everything. However, lawyers are fairly quick to recognize how many legal processes have standardized components – such as completing forms or obtaining follow-up information that, when streamlined, can improve the work product produced and the service delivered to the client. In addition, the rising number of Lean Sigma successes is too significant to ignore. The issue is no longer whether Lean Six Sigma should be considered; it is when and how.

From the client's perspective, it is inconsistent to be told that a firm has decades of deep experience in handling a particular kind of matter and then, in the next breath, have it explained that there is no possible way to predict how long something should take, what could happen at each step, and how much it will cost.

Tim Corcoran, a former CEO, considers this home truth on his Business of Law Blog, in a post addressing recent decisions regarding, among other things, the use of "principal" or "officer" by the Texas State bar that has justifiably raised industry-wide objections.

Corcoran writes that "Business clients are unhappy. Lawyers in the mid-size and big firms that serve us often do a terrible job of communicating. They fail to properly manage expectations by limiting the client's surprise. They tend to treat each matter as if it's unique and infinitely variable, yet at the same time expect us to believe their experience in a given field is meaningful. They believe in charging higher fees based on the length of time they've practiced, even when they are unable or unwilling to demonstrate this experience by using matter budgets or project plans. And their fees are typically established irrespective of the value I place on the services rendered, and what alternatives exist for me to obtain these same services elsewhere, assuming that the seniority of the lawyer and the time necessary to deliver the work are the primary drivers of value. They claim that non-lawyers in a law firm, or worse, non-lawyers providing legal services outside the structure of a law firm, e.g., an LPO, must be incapable of providing quality legal services, even when these alternative providers can unassailably demonstrate higher quality at a lower cost."[3]

The profession is changing

In their September 2012 *Legal Intelligencer* article, Kristin Sudholz (the first chief value officer in any law firm) of Drinker Biddle and Reath LLP and Jennifer Smuts state it bluntly: "Over the last few years, law firms have blamed trends, the economy and even competitors for forcing them to change the way they run their businesses. Ultimately, it doesn't matter where the blame lies – the profession is changing."

Now that clients are frequently presented with alternative options for getting work done rapidly and at greater value, pricing pressures are increasing, and discussion of different fee arrangements is becoming the norm rather than the alternative, we need good processes more than ever. It is essential to determine what clients find valuable in a process, select the lowest cost resource capable of handling each task in the process every time, and then do and deliver the work with the highest standards of quality every time and profitably over all.

As consultants Adam Smith Esq. succinctly put it:

"We [the legal profession] are being squeezed on the top line:

- by clients exercising pricing pressure and
- by the increasing visibility and acceptability of 'substitutes' for at least some of what BigLaw has traditionally done.

We have overcapacity, as an industry, on the order of 7% of our headcount:

- Citi Private Bank has estimated that if all of the 70,000+ lawyers in their sample of firms were working as many hours per year as they did five years ago, 5,000 of them would not be needed

- Yet we continue not only to prevent attrition from taking its natural course, but we are *adding* to [the] headcount.

Expense growth has again begun to outpace revenue growth:

- Our #1 time-tested technique for increasing revenue is to raise rates; we can do that until the cows come home, but clients will take it right back in decreased realization – now at an all-time historic low for the industry

- Our #2 time-tested technique for increasing revenue is to load up on lateral partners; but in this environment they may be adding more to expense than to revenue.

We are completely unserious about taking the shortest route between two points in terms of attacking both overcapacity and expense growth in a single stroke: We have not even begun to address our equity partner headcount.

- Evidently we lack a sense of urgency

- The tepid, 'no longer in free fall' economy has become the *enabling economy*, coyly inviting us to postpone for tomorrow what no longer seems a matter of great urgency today.

- We have, in short, committed the classic and so-oft-repeated sin of wasting a crisis."[4]

Attitude is a choice. So, I encourage firms to view these increased pressures and changes as opportunities to seize: let's not waste a good crisis! There is no better time than now to embrace process improvement. At this point, conversations about this very subject have become much more commonplace between law firms and their clients. It is not just critical for law firms to be able to talk about why process improvement is important to them and what they are doing to build process improvement capability, it can also serve as a significant way to build and enhance relationships. It differentiates a law firm in the marketplace.

The risks are greater than the challenges

Some are skeptical about the ability of law firm management to adapt and lead their organizations through the changes that are going to be required for survival. I have had the repeated good fortune to work with many managing partners, practice group leaders, and business professionals who have embraced process improvement. What I have seen is that their firms do not just "adopt and adapt"; they also develop high-functioning teams, and significant competitive advantages.

Making the necessary changes will not be easy. As Ray Worthy Campbell explains in a 2012 article for the *New York University Journal of Law and Business*, "The business literature on innovation, which has been largely ignored by scholars addressing legal markets, helps make many things clear. Successful incumbents cannot easily change their business model; their resources processes and values are optimized to their current clients and will resist change. Incumbents can use radical new technologies to sustain their business model, but tend to leave alone new technologies or business processes that do not enhance their offerings to their current clients."[5]

However, the risks associated with standing still, while competitors (even those who have yet to appear on the scene) move forward, will be far greater than the challenges firms will inevitably face in embracing process improvement. "Disruptive entrants can enter the low end of the market with new technologies or business processes, and disrupt the market through a sequence that sees them improving their offerings in an iterative manner, eventually allowing them to challenge for the incumbent's best customers." [6]

The pressure to deliver value

A 2014 research report commissioned by Allen & Overy describes how general counsel are responding to external and internal pressures to change the way legal work is delivered – a trend that has picked up significantly since A&O's last survey, two years before: "Since then, the pace of change has accelerated. 86% of the respondents to our latest survey say they are under pressure to deliver more value to their business for less cost. Many legal teams now face increased workloads with headcount and budgets that are cut or frozen. This pressure is forcing legal teams to explore more fundamental change."[7]

General counsel of "one multinational conglomerate", cited in this latest Allen & Overy report, puts the situation for law firms quite simply: "The firms that sit around and think they are going to be able to just continue doing what they have done for the last 100 years are going to become redundant... The model of the provision of legal services is being challenged now more than ever. Law firms have to constantly think about how they are going to innovate and evolve."

As the report notes, "Not all law firms will be able to rise to this challenge, but it is clear that failure to do so carries the risk of not keeping pace with changing client expectations."

These changing expectations include the requirement that firms provide a "one stop shop" for legal services (39 percent of interviewees); 53 percent of respondents in the A&O survey said they "find it challenging to coordinate different types of legal service providers efficiently". Taking heed of the research, the firm reported, "We are deploying technology, business process and project management to combine traditional law firm services and new legal services into hybrid legal solutions."

Gaining buy-in for process improvement

There is no doubt that it is compelling and even inspiring to learn about who is employing process improvement and project management, and how and where those firms and law departments have been successful. Another key point that helps to make the case for Lean Six Sigma is to highlight the fact that one of our goals in fundamentally changing our processes is to create even greater opportunities for lawyers to focus on the areas where they contribute the highest value, which are practicing law and applying strategic thinking to legal problems. This takes advantage of their experience and training by removing waste by reducing time spent on administrative tasks that irritate them and other non-value-adding activities. It is critical to show that when we improve processes, lawyers will still have plenty of latitude and flexibility, since we never gratuitously standardize any part of a process or crudely suggest that improving efficiency is as simple as reducing headcount.

This is especially important where business professionals who are not practicing lawyers are responsible for leading the charge. Notice that we *do not* use the term "non-lawyer". The practice of referring to professional staff by what they *do not* do is not just one of the unique and negative aspects of the legal profession; it is also, arguably, a violation of the Lean Sigma principle to align and empower employees.

UK-based law firm asb law, which has offices in Crawley, Sussex, and Maidstone, Kent, provides an example where all employees are integrated. According to its mission statement, the firm seeks "to continuously improve our internal processes so that we operate efficiently and, ultimately, make cost, resource and time savings". In order to facilitate the goal of continuous improvement, "Everyone at asb law is encouraged to challenge the established way of doing things and to suggest improvements. Lean Champions from each team help to coordinate and share ideas across the firm, and lean targets are written into performance measures."

Through this, the firm asserts that "over recent years, we've become quite adept at improving the efficiency and cost-effectiveness of our operations. Our employees are actively involved in questioning not only how we work internally, but also how our clients and suppliers might improve their services. Indeed, we're collaborating with several business clients to help them apply lean techniques to manage risk."

"Working collaboratively also demonstrates congruent beliefs and a commitment to responding to client feedback," says Amy Hrehovcik of Ailey Advisors. She points to the 2014 ACC Survey, which reports that 89 percent of chief legal officers recognize the importance of professional development in advancing non-legal skills among their staff. The non-legal skills most sought after include business management (62 percent), project management (54 percent), and communication (49 percent).

Additionally, early success is important for beginning to build momentum and achieving "buy in" for the initiative as a whole. It is a truism that no organization has a second chance to do something right the first time, so selecting the right baseline or demonstration project that will serve as your firm's own case study will always provide the most convincing evidence that "Lean Sigma works here".

Linking quality and performance

Lawyers, and rightfully so, care a great deal about quality, and often express concern that it will be sacrificed by making a process more efficient. They also worry that profitability will suffer. "One of the first solid pieces of evidence linking quality and business results was groundbreaking research performed by PIMS (Profit Impact of Market Strategy). Over a period of years PIMS amassed a large database documenting the strategies and financial results of more than 450 companies and nearly 3,000 business units in order to study the general relationships between strategy and company performance. Its purpose was not to prove a link between quality and profitability (or between any other particular business strategy and firm performance), but rather to discover those strategic principles most strongly related to performance. Among all the strategic principles distilled from the PIMS studies, one linkage between strategy and performance stood out above all the rest: quality.

A quality edge boosts performance in the short run by allowing the firm to charge premium prices, and in the long run by enabling growth of the firm through both market expansion and gains in market share. PIMS found that businesses offering superior product/service quality are more profitable than those with inferior quality, based on two key measurements: return on sales and return on investment. In addition to these profitability and growth advantages, PIMS also revealed other benefits of superior perceived quality: "stronger customer loyalty, more repeat purchases, less vulnerability to price wars, and lower marketing costs".[8]

In short, focusing on quality can help make a very compelling case for trying process improvement. Lean Sigma has provided particularly good quality case studies. This is due to the framework of process improvement and a focus on delivering bottom-line results.

Technology and process improvement

As might be expected, technology is in and of itself a sort of process improvement. When there is an upgrade on a device, for example, it usually presents us with a better way of doing something. These days, we are alerted to upgrades to all our applications with such frequency that it is now common to, quite literally, wake up to process improvement.

While technology is nearly always a part of the solution to improving a process, to a process improvement practitioner, technology alone may often appear to be a solution looking for a problem. It really depends on how we frame what we are trying to solve. For example, if we describe the situation as "we don't have a CRM system", then the only response to the problem is to select, install, and roll out a new kind of technology – a client relationship management (CRM) system. If, instead, we take a process improvement approach and characterize our problem as "we are not capturing firm experience, which is impacting our ability to compete for new work, engage in client development activities, and manage our business processes such as firm mailings", we start to think about all the elements – in addition to technologies like CRM – that will help us address the problem and seize attendant opportunities.

In an opinion piece in *Managing Partner* magazine entitled "Efficiency – your starter for 10", Simon Slater, managing director of First Counsel Consulting Limited and a founding member of the Legal Practice Group, wrote: "The legal service reforms will pave the way for new entrants to the market and competition the likes of which law firms have not yet seen. For many firms the key to survival in the new legal landscape will be investment in efficiency, but where exactly should that investment be made?"

Slater highlighted a small, progressive law firm: "'A single key decision we made recently will be the difference between survival and failure,' said the [firm's] managing partner... His board's decision was to invest no less than £400,000 in technology to streamline its processes and improve the delivery of legal services. When probed, he said the firm could only succeed by becoming truly efficient. Intelligent deployment of technology was the key."

Therefore, Slater advises that firms "Use the right technology to support the streamlining of processes in the delivery of legal advice and client services. Don't over-engineer and recognise that all services commoditise in time... Support the increased dependence on technology with an investment in training for your people. Help them embrace change and new working practices positively." When it comes to Lean Six Sigma, Slater advises firms to "adopt [the] thinking without the dogma. Six Sigma is simply a process used to identify and eradicate defects in manufacturing... On a smaller scale, the same philosophy can be adapted to precedents, knowledge and legal processes... Think about lean management. Law firms are fundamentally simple businesses, but they are often over-managed. Keep management small and 'local'. Consider partial outsourcing, but with care. Control directly what you must. The key test? Is the value people add greater than the paper they push?"

The rate of change is not slowing down. So, if your processes are not changing as fast as the environment is changing, as former General Electric CEO Jack Welch would say, "the end is in sight". The changes in the business environment create ever greater requirements for higher process capabilities and higher process efficiencies. We have extremely talented and capable people working in law firms in all sorts of positions. But they are working with processes that do not allow them to function to their highest levels. Instead, legal and business professionals in law firms are sometimes coping with processes that are horribly broken; at the Legal Lean Sigma Institute, we routinely suggest that when you put talented people up against a broken process, the process will always win.

So, talent acquisition and retention, competitors, technology, employees, regulations, and most importantly, clients are all part of the driving forces that are creating widening performance gaps in the processes in law firms. Because our processes are not capable, errors are made and waste occurs. Then, we spend time addressing those mistakes, making corrections, pacifying people, and recovering. As a result, it is difficult for anyone to have the time to improve anything. We call this being stuck in the "fire-fighting doom loop".

For law firms, the two most compelling drivers for process improvement are clients and the competition (other firms and legal service providers). We leverage the realizations associated with those drivers to convince law firms of the importance of "pulling the car over and finally fixing the engine rather than continuing to drive or attempting to repair it as we speed down the highway". Process improvement is an excellent way to get out of this "doom loop".

The DuPont Legal Model

In terms of clients driving these changes, DuPont is the most widely known and highly regarded legal department driving efficiency via the DuPont Legal Model, now 22 years old. DuPont's website states that: "Part of the success of the DuPont Legal Model is its ability to embrace change and adapt to new challenges. In order to continually integrate new strategies and solutions into the DuPont Legal Model, DuPont Legal, its Primary Law Firms (PLFs) and Primary Service Providers (PSPs) have devoted considerable time and money to applying the Six Sigma methodology to processes within the legal department's realm. Six Sigma provides a disciplined approach to business improvement by systematically improving processes and eliminating defects, which are defined as units that are not members of the intended population.

Six Sigma at DuPont Legal has led to savings, process accountability and much more. At the outset, there was little experience in the business world for Six Sigma in legal services. The drive for collaboration and bottom line savings in the Legal Model served as an important grounding.

Within DuPont Legal, early projects addressed:

- Litigation costs
- Patents and trademarks
- Administrative services

- Information technology implementation
- Records management

Six Sigma supports the unique role that the Legal Function provides in its delivery of legal services to the corporation. Aligning with the accomplishment of short- and long-term strategic goals, the Legal Six Sigma adds:

- Support for process excellence in core legal processes
- Adherence to cost effective Control Plans
- The opportunity to identify and lead cross functional projects
- The management of legal risks of the corporation

Today, every global member of DuPont Legal and every PLF and PSP plays a part in Six Sigma. It is the way work is done at DuPont Legal and key to meeting the company's 'Sustainable Growth' productivity goal. Given the Legal Network members' central role in cost savings and risk management, their continued and active involvement is critical to the program's success."[9]

Clients expect efficient processes

Today, many clients' requests for proposals (RFPs) and information ask firms to describe their process improvement or process management programs. RFPs seem to be increasingly focused on understanding how law firms are becoming more efficient – and how the firms suggest, given their knowledge of Lean and Six Sigma, that the clients themselves can be more efficient.

To be clear, today's clients not only expect their law firms to understand and employ process improvement methodologies in their own work, they also expect them to provide recommendations as to how they can help the client in the same vein. This requires that the lawyers and business professionals in law firms – whether they are client facing or not – be able to identify and propose ideas for improvements. Without the language and tools of Lean and Six Sigma deployed on a more institutional basis, this becomes increasingly more difficult, particularly as the work, services, and number and depth of relationships grows between firm and client.

Here are just a few examples from RFPs:

- Please address how you will accomplish greater efficiencies. For example, do you employ project management techniques such as Six Sigma or Lean?

- How and why should Company A have confidence that your firm will handle matters efficiently and in a cost-effective manner without sacrificing quality?

- What changes could Company A implement to make your work for us more cost-efficient?

- Company A seeks reliable, financially stable law firms that can meet stringent cost, quality, and service requirements. A team will evaluate each proposal based on various criteria, including, but not limited to processes generating operational efficiencies.

When competing these days, using smoke and mirrors to respond to specific questions about how your firm is approaching efficiency and employing Lean and Six Sigma will not only be ineffective, but could potentially harm your firm's position and reputation.

These days, there is an increasing need to "get legal procurement's attention", according to Dr Silvia Hodges Silverstein,[10] whose research and work in procurement is setting the standard, and who has provided a chapter on that topic for this book (see Chapter 6).

"Procurement is now involved in the purchasing of legal services and it's quickly becoming the 'new normal'. Larger corporations in particular engage procurement, not only for sourcing low-end, routine, or commoditized legal services, but increasingly for higher-stakes legal work as well. But that doesn't mean that law firms or in-house legal and procurement teams are well equipped to deal with this new landscape and to make these new relationships successful.

Legal procurement analyzes many things that might not have been given a lot of attention in the legal profession before: Industry bench-marking analysis is conducted by 71 percent of respondents in the survey, followed by rate increase analysis and invoice audits (67 percent each). Half of the respondents forecast budgets, followed by alternative fee arrangement analysis, and key performance indicator analysis.

Procurement also embraces legal spend management (75 percent) and e-billing (71 percent). Contract database for legal, matter management and in-house e-discovery are used by 40 to 50 percent of respondents in the survey. Firms' project management and process improvement capabilities are increasingly important: 48 percent of respondents in the survey deemed them 'very important', another 16 percent as 'important'."

Uptake of Lean Six Sigma in law firms

David Skinner, a certified Lean Six Sigma Sensei with over 20 years of experience of practicing law in law firms and as in-house counsel in Canada and overseas suggests: "It may be that firms in the UK and Australia are slightly ahead of the curve because they've already adapted business structures that are more conducive to a business-like approach. Let's face it: a huge partnership is hard to manage. If you have to get 900 partners in ten different cities in six countries around the world on board, it's going to take you a while. Smaller firms are more agile and more able to adapt and that's where we see a huge uptake."[11]

With that in mind, it is interesting to read a survey from several years ago that is available from Altman Weil and which includes data on the use of Six Sigma by US law firms. The study found that:

- Three firms or 5.1 percent, had utilized Six Sigma;
- Five firms or 8.5 percent had not used Six Sigma but planned to in the future;
- 51 firms, or 86.4 percent, had not used Six Sigma and had no plans to do so.[12]

Originally developed by Motorola, Six Sigma's value has been proven in companies such as AlliedSignal, Sony, General Electric, Lockheed Martin, Boeing, Verizon, and IBM, just to name a few. Given the success already achieved by many (client) companies as well as law firms who had by now implemented Lean Six Sigma and reported great results, I was astonished that more had not yet utilized the methodology. Things began to change very soon, however.

By September 2008, Seyfarth Shaw, with their emphasis on branding the firm based on experience and results, became a driving force behind change at firms competing against them for clients.

When Altman Weil released their 2014 survey, the contrast to the 2008 responses was dramatic. "More than 90% of firm leaders have said they believe there is a permanent market shift requiring greater efficiency in the delivery of legal services.

- In the area of efficient legal service delivery, 54% of the large firm group was pursuing change, compared to 34% of the smaller firms

- 43% of firms offer PM training.
- Only 30% of law firms have taken on the really challenging task of re-engineering work processes."[13]

With 70 percent of firms not yet reporting that they have had either the interest or the fortitude to employ process improvement, there is still plenty of room in the marketplace for those who are interested in beginning to explore this now – and it is a wise idea to do so while it remains an option, not a requirement. Often, it is the risk and cost associated with not doing something that can provide the most compelling reason to act. Consider this: according to an American Bar Association study released in 2012, 30 percent of legal malpractice suits were the result of administrative errors, including failure to calendar or react to calendar items, and lost files, documents, or evidence. What would happen if your firm decides to do nothing about efficiency?

"As there is a relationship between cost and price, there exists a relationship between process and cost. How a firm performs services impacts cost. Performance is indelibly tied to process/workflow. This is true even in the practice of law."[14] With all of the internal and external pressures to be more efficient and a keen interest from partners in remaining profitable, it is certain that a specific role that is focused on process improvement will become another business function in a law firm that is the rule rather than the exception. The increased number of those responsible for process improvement, project management and/or pricing suggests that this will occur sooner rather than later.

Award-winning examples of process improvement in action

Important drivers causing increasing interest in Lean and Six Sigma by law firms are the significant marketing and business development opportunities, along with competition and award-winning ideas, programs, and innovations from other law firms. Examples include those mentioned below.

Baker Donelson

One of the first firms in the US to invest in the development of its own legal project management (LPM) system, Baker Donelson received ILTA'S 2012 Distinguished Peer Award for outstanding achievements in the category of "Project of the Year".

The firm states that its system "is an industry leading and patent pending system which can be implemented in any type of engagement – business or litigation… Baker Donelson also formed a Legal Project Management Office (LPMO) to provide support for the BakerManage system and guide the implementation of project management principles across the Firm… The goals of BakerManage include: Evaluate legal processes across the Firm to create guidelines for attorneys which promote consistency, encourage appropriate resource assignment, omit duplication and streamline delivery."

The Hunoval Law Firm

Based in Charlotte, North Carolina, the foreclosure firm was one of five finalists for the "Best Process Improvement Project" at the 15th annual PEX awards, along with Capital One and Pitney Bowes (the winner). Hunoval, a firm set up from scratch in 2009, was nominated for its implementation of Six Sigma principles in a legal environment. According to Hunoval, "this is not about change in how we practice law. It's about law practice management, improving the business side – an idea that is changing how law firms can be run." What is more, these are changes that appeal directly to how clients run their own businesses: "When they hear us speaking that same language," Hunoval says, "I can see the lightbulb moment where the client or potential client says, 'Oh my God, here's a lawyer who actually gets it.'"[15]

Littler's CaseSmart program

Littler's CaseSmart program has been recognized for creating an efficient and novel way of approaching equal employment opportunity (EEO) and employment litigation work, redesigning the processes to eliminate inefficiencies and inconsistencies. According to the firm's website, "Littler CaseSmart was developed by legal practice management professionals and tenured employment lawyers, all focused on innovation for the purpose of controlling costs and delivering real client value." The firm's innovative approach won a 2012 College of Law Practice Management InnovAction award and a 2011 ILTA Project of the Year award. The firm already has a solid track record of experience with CaseSmart, having "successfully handled more than 9,000 charges within the Littler CaseSmart model".

The real innovation that came from carefully and thoroughly mapping out their processes for these kinds of work allowed Littler to develop software that automates and tracks entire processes, which provides their clients with a privileged and sophisticated view of all matters. Littler points out that "The client dashboard provides matter-level data across an entire set of matters, including the ability to filter by type of charge, type of case, location, date range, status, response type, and other criteria. The client dashboard also allows users to drill into specific matters and to view all substantive documents, matter summaries, and intake data. Moreover, your company's preferences for communication protocols, frequency and types of reporting are configurable in the Littler CaseSmart solution."

Seyfarth Shaw

SeyfarthLean has been the subject of numerous articles and representatives from the firm have delivered a multitude of programs and published pieces concerning their broad-based, leading approach to process improvement. In 2011 International Legal Technology Association recognized the firm twice with the Innovative Law Firm of the Year award and Innovative Project of the Year award. The following year, Seyfarth received the College of Law Practice Management's InnovAction Award.

The marketing opportunities that a focus on process improvement generates are significant. Seyfarth Shaw branded its approach "Seyfarth*Lean*", developing a serious competitive advantage and generating a high-visibility campaign around its message about using Lean Six Sigma and project management to drive value for clients. This was a firm that embraced the idea of being first, rather than waiting to see who else would follow, thereby raising the bar for all law firms (whether or not they were pursuing the same clients).

The firm designed a marketing campaign around its work and skill sets that continues to be very effective. Thus, Seyfarth uses the competitive advantages that Lean and Six Sigma can deliver very well. With a program to develop deep skills and projects across the firm, they had real results to include in their award applications, branding, marketing, communications, and business development efforts. As such, they were way ahead of the market and became known for their leadership in efficiency.

Squire Sanders

The firm was recognized in 2012 in *Law Technology News* with the Most Innovative Use of Technology in a Large Law Firm award for their Intelligent Discovery Process™, an e-discovery project management and technology platform that leverages disciplined management, predictive coding, and other technology to improve efficiencies in the e-discovery process. The *Law Technology News* award distinguishes Squire Sanders as a leader in the convergence of technology and the law and recognizes its practical application to provide clients with more efficient, cost-effective, and defensible results.

The firm's press materials state that "Squire Sanders was early to recognize the potential of predictive coding and technology assisted review processes. 'We're not just talking about predictive coding, we're using it as part of a disciplined process to deliver better, more cost efficient and defensible results to our clients', said Scott A. Kane, Chair of Squire Sanders' eDiscovery & Data Management Practice. 'Our investment in the Squire Sanders Intelligent Discovery Process™ has paid off not only in terms of client review costs, but also in terms of quality, strategic decision-making and budgeting accuracy.'"

Foley & Lardner

Another approach law firms are taking is to take direct part in a client's own process improvement activities. Nowhere are there greater opportunities to do this than in firms with manufacturing clients.

A supreme example is provided by Foley & Lardner, which was recognized by the Legal Marketing Association (LMA) with the 2014 Your Honor Award in Practice Development. The award recognized the firm's launch of the Legal Innovation Hubsm for NextGen manufacturers, a firm-wide business development and marketing program devoted to next-generation manufacturing. The hub is comprised of a dedicated network of departments, industry teams, and practice groups and helps manufacturing clients engage in dialogues and tackle the transformational issues associated with next-generation manufacturing.

"Foley has been serving U.S. manufacturers for nearly 175 years, and this is an industry we know well", said Janis Nordstrom, Foley's global chief business strategies officer. "As a result of this program, we are strengthening our reputation as the 'go-to firm' for next-gen manufacturers, helping them collaborate on the legal and business challenges presented by the convergence of technology and manufacturing."

References

1. Dalton, K. and Dugga, J., "Lean and agile: How legal project management can transform client services", *Managing Partner* online, 25 March 2013.
2. Sager, T. L., and Winkelman, S. L., "Six Sigma: Positioning for Competitive Advantage", ACCA Docket 19 (No. 1), 2001.

3. Corcoran, T. B., "Bar Associations: Protecting Consumers or the Status Quo?" (blog post), *Corcoran Law Biz Blog*, 2 July 2014; see http://www.corcoranlawbizblog. com/2014/07/protecting-the-status-quo/.

4. Adam Smith Esq., "The Enabling Economy: The Essay" published 26 August 2013; see www.adamsmithesq.com/2013/08/the-enabling-economy-the-essay/?single.

5. Campbell, R. W., "Rethinking Regulation and Innovation in the U.S. Legal Services Market", *New York University Journal of Law & Business*, vol. 9, no. 1, Fall 2012; www.nyujlb.org/wp-content/uploads/nyb_9-1-1_scissored.7-76.pdf.

6. Ibid.

7. Allen & Overy Global Survey, "Unbundling a market: The appetite for new legal services models", May 2014; see www.allenovery.com/SiteCollectionDocuments/ global-survey-lsm.pdf.

8. Ryan, J., "Making the Case for Economic Quality, a White Paper for The American Society for Quality (ASQ)"; see http://asq.org/economic-case.

9. See www.dupontlegalmodel.com.

10. Silverstein, S.H., "Get legal procurement's attention" (blog post), 19 May 2014.

11. Skinner, D. and Skinner, K., "Who says there's no messing with lawyers?", Process Excellence Network, 9 March 2013; see www.processexcellencenetwork. com/lean-six-sigma-business-transformation/articles/who-says-there-s-no-messing-with-lawyers.

12. Altman Weil Inc, "Results Altman Weil 2005 Survey of Major Law Firm Management Techniques"; see www.altmanweil.com/dir_docs/resource/ b9ca8e17-6530-446d-bb8d-62a2376c4602_document.pdf.

13. Altman Weil Inc, "2014 Law Firms in Transition: An Altman Weil Flash Survey"; see www.altmanweil.com/dir_docs/resource/f68236ab-d51f-4d81-8172-96e8d47387e3_document.pdf.

14. Kubicki, J., and Wood, C., "Business Design for Law Firms, Part 2", Commentary on Legal Transformation Institute online, 3 July 2014; see http://legal transformationinstitute.com/blog/2014/7/3/business-design-for-law-firms-part-2.

15. Carter, T., "Foreclosure firm goes statistical to improve speed and quality", *American Bar Association Journal* online, see www.abajournal.com/magazine/ article/foreclosure_firm_goes_statistical_to_improve_speed_and_quality.

Chapter 3:
DMAIC – The framework

Lean Sigma uses a disciplined problem solving approach known as DMAIC, which stands for define, measure, analyze, improve, and control. This acronym is practically a mantra for process improvement practitioners and provides the framework for a process improvement project. After a project is prioritized and resourced, a good process improvement methodology must be used to deliver results reliably and following the DMAIC project execution methodology significantly improves the probability of project success.

DMAIC provides us with a prescribed sequence of steps that includes helpful ways of thinking through and analyzing many business questions and situations. We are encouraged to specifically define the problem or opportunity, gather data, analyze it, and only then to consider solutions. A more typical approach seems to be that we leap from having a fairly general notion of a situation to selecting a solution (and getting a bit stubborn about it) very quickly. As most people realize, this approach involves a great deal of guesswork. While it is inexpensive to guess, it can be very expensive (and a colossal waste of time) to guess wrong.

The five steps of DMAIC
The five DMAIC steps of define, measure, analyze, improve, and control are always performed in that exact sequence, without ever skipping steps.

1. **Define** the problem and why it needs to be solved – Here is where we carefully work through all the elements of a project charter;

2. **Measure** the current performance of the process – We measure the process in two dimensions: the performance level, or how well the process meets client expectations (process performance), and the resource requirements, or the time, people, equipment, etc., needed to carry out the process (process efficiency);

3. **Analyze** the opportunities to reduce waste or variation, identifying root causes;

4. **Improve** the process by developing solutions and identifying, implementing, and validating process changes; and

5. **Control** the process by implementing methods to ensure improvements will be sustainable and that the improvements are translated into benefits.

DMAIC also includes change management, communication, and avoidance of failure through the effective use of safeguards that are built into the framework. These safeguards include the all-important meetings with a steering committee, which follow the conclusion of each phase. This ensures that we are communicating as we progress with our projects and that we are employing good change management techniques.

Thus, after (and sometimes during) each phase, the process improvement project team meets with the project sponsor and a steering committee that is typically comprised of cross-functional leaders in the firm to pass through "gate reviews" or "toll gates". In these meetings, the steering committee holds the team responsible for completing specific deliverables that are required in each phase and ensures the team has addressed all the important considerations. They also offer additional perspective, information, suggestions, and feedback.

Thus, rather than complete a project from start to finish and then deliver the results, the approach demanded by process improvement is for our cross-functional and diverse team to regularly check-in with their project sponsor and engage in gate reviews with a group of decision makers that stays with the project from start to finish. This format builds in regular and ongoing communication for the duration of the project and provides a forum for the team to share their work as it progresses from diagnosing, measuring, and analyzing the process to finally developing improvement ideas. The shareholders also have opportunities to contribute their diverse perspectives, expertise, and resources on an ongoing basis – this is built in to the process of process improvement.

DMAIC builds in failure avoidance due to its design and rigor. It incorporates change management principles to ensure consensus is built as the project team progresses through each phase. Thus, there are numerous benefits to following the framework and to never skipping steps.

Step 1: Define

In the "define" phase, we will identify a serious business issue, one that is worthy of allocating resources to address. We initiate the project and carefully select and form the team. In the define phase, the project team will create and approve a project charter, working through each element, including the project plan. There have been occasions where teams working on a project have been unable to convince themselves that the project they have been asked to deliver is addressing something important enough to prioritize and resource. When that happens, realizing this fact early saves the firm more than time and resources – it prevents a firm from having a poor outcome or experience as the result of the process improvement efforts.

Because it is so important, Lean Sigma Principle 1, "specify value in the eyes of the client", is addressed at the very beginning of the project. In order to do so, we must also identify client requirements with tools such as "voice of the client", "moments of truth", "critical to quality", and a "client requirements summary". Finally, we will document the process using an "IPO (input, process, output) Diagram" (some organizations use SIPOC, which stands for suppliers, inputs, process, outputs, customer).

In addition to making sure that the project addresses an important client or business need, we employ good project management skills from the outset, making sure that the project scope and expectations are clear, that there is strong sponsorship and ownership, and that the problem (and the impact of the solution) can be measured and quantified. The team also begins to determine the most useful problem-solving approaches for the problem.

Step 2: Measure

In the "measure" phase, we concentrate on Lean Sigma Principle 2: "Identify waste and variation by mapping and measuring the process". Thus, one of our first tasks is to map the process, using one or more of a variety of process map types. In this way, we gain a thorough understanding of the current state of our process (how we do things now); therefore, the team must have the ability to do both basic process mapping (IPO, block, top-down, detailed) and specialized mapping (swim lane map, spaghetti diagram, information flow diagram, time-value analysis), each of which shows the same process from a different vantage point.

A block diagram, for example, shows the whole process in just a few, key steps, while a top-down map shows sub-tasks under the main blocks. A detailed map shows all the steps with their relationships to all the other steps, including those that are wasteful, such as waiting and re-work. Specialized process maps are created to highlight particular kinds of issues or waste, such as handoffs, which are good places to start, since waste always accrues at boundaries. The goal is to capture the steps and thought processes, especially reviews and decision points, in a process.

Obviously, process maps are excellent tools for communications with clients and teams. They also allow for expedient onboarding of any new members and support business development efforts by engaging prospective clients, referral sources, and strategic partners in conversations that elicit points of collaboration and differentiation. Typically, as soon as a process map is developed, teams immediately identify specific areas for improvement.

In the measure phase, the team also establishes a baseline of performance against which to measure progress, and measures many things in and about the process to identify waste and variation, defects, and causes of defects.

Then, we develop a measurement strategy and plan, using tools such as an issue diagram and/or measurement assessment tree. These tools allow the team to discuss what we want to measure in a structured format. Then, we attempt to gather information related to what we are interested in learning. We sometimes describe this gathering step as a big "fishing expedition" to see what can be learned and what is available. It is an iterative process to gather data, since a team might be (and often is) surprised by what is and what is not currently available in a firm either in terms of ease of access, quantity, or quality.

There is a hierarchy of data with respect to its usefulness and validity:

1. Reliable data that can be extracted from a system in electronic format;

2. Data that exists, but not in a convenient format (for example, paper files), which requires the team to figure out where it is, extract it, and then put it into a useful format, such as a spreadsheet;

3. Data that does not yet exist, but can be created using observation worksheets, surveys, and log sheets;

4. Externally available data, which usually is not specific to the firm, but may still be useful;

5. Estimations and opinion, which is better than nothing but not ideal. Usually, this involves asking several knowledgeable people and collating opinions; and

6.   Anecdotes, which might be useful as a last resort. However, we have to be sure to understand the frequency of any occurrence rather than relying on one person's perception or experience.[1]

While the deep analysis of your data will take place in the next phase ("analyze"), long before that the team will need to understand what the data means and whether it has answered the questions raised so far in the project. Creating a visual representation of data is a powerful first step toward understanding, so each different data point that is collected is turned into charts and graphs (like Pareto charts, run charts, and histograms) to help the team consider all the information. Graphical data analysis is the process of making sense of the data, determining if it is adequate, and representing it in a way that informs and highlights key information. Thus, all the data that is gathered allows the team to begin describing the current state of the process very clearly and accurately; this is usually the first time a firm has ever truly understood how a process has been performing. Typically, it is very eye opening.

At this point in the project, a team will have a lot of data about the process, including process maps showing steps and waste, characterization data showing overall process capability and efficiency along several dimensions, and stratification data showing patterns and providing clues to causes. At this point, the team is ready to summarize and prioritize our areas of opportunity into a limited number of "focus areas" the team has become most interested in analyzing in greater detail in the next phase.

Finally, we use our graphical displays to help us create a storyboard that explains our logic to the steering committee. Now, the team is ready for another gate review. At this point in the project, the walls of the room in which the team is working are becoming increasingly covered with graphics, flip chart papers, and sticky notes. As such, it is ideal if the steering committee is able to be on site for this gate review.

Step 3: Analyze
In "analyze", we examine each focus area to identify and verify waste, defects, and determine root causes. Root cause analysis takes place in three steps:

1.   Exploring;
2.   Generating hypotheses; and
3.   Verifying causes.

We use the data gathered in the measure phase to find patterns, trends, and other differences that suggest or support theories about the causes of waste or defects. We may need to gather further data to complete our analysis.

Our first step is to explore each focus area. We begin by assembling all the process maps and analyses that relate to each focus area. Using the Lean perspective, the team annotates each process map with notes highlighting non-value-adding steps, waste, potential causes of problems, and ideas for further exploration. All process maps are useful for asking whether steps are non-value-adding. In particular, the team looks for disconnects, decision points, inspection points, redundancies, and rework loops – and begins to illustrate why process maps can be such terrific tools to use in conversations with clients, prospective clients, and referral sources.

The team takes a similar approach to the graphical analyses, annotating each graph with notes about interesting observations, patterns, and trends. Finally, the team determines whether other tools or analyses might be useful in exploring the focus areas, and for each focus area, creates a summary of interesting observations and questions created in this "explore" step.

The second step is to generate hypotheses for the causes of the waste or defects. At the end of the explore step, the team has a list of interesting observations, waste, problems, and questions. To find the root cause for defects, we use tools such as "5 Whys" and/or cause-and-effect diagrams (also known as fishbone diagrams).

Lastly, the team uses data to verify or discard its hypotheses about causes. The team is then ready for its next gate review, having examined Focus Areas for bottlenecks, disconnects, and redundancies that might contribute to waste, analyzed data to understand potential root causes of problems and defects, developed root cause hypotheses for problems, and then investigated and verified root cause hypotheses to isolate a "vital few" root causes.

Finally, the team gets to improve the process. At this point, it is (hopefully) clear how important it is to never skip steps in the DMAIC approach. If we were to begin to develop solutions too early, we most certainly would not identify the best solutions that are most able to provide us with the greatest improvement opportunities.

Step 4: Improve

In the "improve" phase, the team generates and develops creative solutions that address the root causes confirmed in the analyze phase. Tools such as problem statements, solutions filter, structured brainstorming techniques, and tree diagrams are used at this point.

Then, the team analyzes options and selects the best one, using a force field analysis, pros and cons analysis, a weighted decision matrix, or an impact/ease matrix. After planning and executing a pilot test, the team conducts an after-action review. After an interim review with the steering committee and making refinements based on a pilot test, the firm is ready to implement full-scale improvements with detailed action planning, communication, training, troubleshooting, and ongoing measurement and performance measurement.

Step 5: Control

In the "control" phase, the process improvement project team develops approaches to maintain a process with an operation that is stable, predictable, and meets client requirements. This involves documenting the new process using tools such as standard operating procedures or statements of work, which describe how each step in the process will be performed, ideally in a standardized way.

All key project materials and artifacts should be preserved in a project repository, which ensures appropriate and ongoing availability of information about what has been done and what results were achieved by the project. Processes will always relate to, or overlap with, others in the firm, so those involved in other, future projects will undoubtedly find the team's work of interest. A project repository will explain the thought process behind your process improvements, and should follow the DMAIC flow of your project so that it can serve as a knowledge resource for the firm.

The team must complete the project by designing the controls, and defining metrics, responsibilities, and corrective actions. The project is finished when the firm has instituted process ownership to ensure that the benefits of the work are captured and the overall performance of the process is being monitored. The process owner has ultimate responsibility for maintaining the improvements achieved and educates others about the reasons for maintaining the improvements and the benefits derived from these. This person manages control and knows whether a process is performing adequately; if it is not, they are responsible for planning improvements.

Finally, the team compiles results data, confirming the achievement of the project charter goal. It will be important to report accomplishments, to open issues to senior management – and to celebrate success!

The Kaizen approach

In addition to DMAIC for full-scale projects, law firms I work with are seeing good results with the Kaizen approach. In the Lean Sigma world, Kaizen has come to mean a focused, fast, structured process improvement methodology. We think of a Kaizen as an accelerated problem-solving methodology, useful for problems of limited scope. We still go through the normal DMAIC sequence, but do so in a condensed time period, which makes it an ideal approach for firms with busy people on teams who do not typically all work in the same office.

One team member involved in a Kaizen project reported that "overall, the process worked well. I liked the Kaizen approach. The time frame/commitment worked well for me. After hearing tales of the prior (full scale DMAIC) projects and time involved in those I was very pleased to be involved with a Kaizen approach."

The way we structure our Kaizens is to begin with a call to prepare for our first team gathering, and then having a kick-off meeting, when we will carry out the "define" stage and plan the "measure" stage. The team then spends about a month collecting data and then comes back together for a three-day Kaizen workshop, where we will carry out as much of the remaining DMAIC sequence as we can, reviewing all the data and selecting focus areas on the first day (measure), then discussing causes and interrelationships (analyze) and developing solution alternatives and recommendations, plus implementing these as far as possible in the workshop (improve). The team continues to work on implementation and developing control schemes (improve and control phases) after the workshop, when working together effectively is less dependent on being in the same room at the same time.

In addition to providing us with a logical sequence of steps that have plenty of change management and communications built into the process, the DMAIC framework helps us to minimize or even eliminate typical project failures. It also helps us avoid the typical causes of poor achievement of promised results. To illustrate the point:

- Define helps us avoid picking the wrong problem to solve in the first place by having the team to carefully define what it is they are trying to solve, determine the scope, and so forth;
- The measure phase greatly improves our chances of selling our recommendations;
- Analyze safeguards against making poor recommendations; and

- The improve phase helps to ensure we develop the right solutions and avoid poor implementation.

Team members who started out as Six Sigma Yellow Belts and then earned their Green Belts after successfully completing their projects have this to say about the DMAIC framework:

- "Working as a team to improve a process allows you to collect a large amount of data, see different perspectives, and complete tasks more efficiently. DMAIC works."
- "Breaking down the project using the define, measure, analyze, improve, and control process really does work. It seems a bit overwhelming at first, but it gives a great result."

References

1. "Outlining the problem of long delays, CIO Kevin Divine of the Hunoval Law Firm asked supervisors and staff in the firm's North Carolina default department how long they thought it took from file intake to sending out a notice of hearing to launch the foreclosure process. Anecdotally, they saw it as 14 to 20 days. But the crunched numbers tallied 69." See Carter, T., "Foreclosure firm goes statistical to improve speed and quality", *American Bar Association Journal* online; www.abajournal.com/magazine/article/ foreclosure_firm_goes_statistical_to_improve_speed_and_quality.

Chapter 4:
Systematic approaches

Lean Six Sigma programs have a place on a continuum; they vary in scope and depth and in effectiveness and impact. Opportunistic improvements are excellent places to begin employing Lean and Six Sigma. However, to really improve processes to their maximum potential, firms benefit the most from employing a systematic, structured approach whereby all key processes are included. A firm that embraces a systematic approach also employs a wide range of Six Sigma and Lean tools in an appropriate sequence.

This approach requires a longer-term investment that takes time to deliver benefits – but it offers significant returns. In a corporate setting, one of the best-known systematic process improvement success stories is that of the General Electric Company, which made Six Sigma a foundation of GE strategy and a fundamental element of the company's business approach under its former chairman, Jack Welch. GE's Six Sigma initiative began in 1995 with 200 projects delivering little to no financial benefit to the company, and then expanded within two years to 6,000 projects delivering $320 million in productivity gains and profits. By 1999, GE was publicly claiming $2 billion in annual benefits, and by 2001 the company reported that 500,000 Six Sigma projects had been completed since the start of the initiative.

There are many other excellent examples that help to explain why a systematic approach is so powerful (and which also shed light on the expectations of legal departments and corporate clients of law firms and the kind of disconnect that very often exists with regard to their outside counsel):

- AlliedSignal, for example, is also known for its successes with Six Sigma, which the company reports has saved it $1.5 billion since 1991.

- Ford Motor Company started its Six Sigma effort in 2000 and, in 2003, stated that it had saved $1 billion through waste elimination, experiencing record improvement in its "Things Gone Wrong". A year later, to the figure had doubled due, primarily, to waste reduction and process improvements, rather than through cost avoidance.

- Samsung Electronics Company, which also launched a Six Sigma initiative in 2000, projected "cumulative financial benefits of $1.5 billion through the end of 2002. These benefits include cost savings and increased profits from sales and new product development. Its Six Sigma projects also are credited with an average of 50 percent reduction in defects."[1]

For many years, legal services seemed to be excused from the same requirements the business world had of products and other service businesses. It should be abundantly clear that this is no longer the case. For there is nothing inherently different about the practice of law that exempts a law firm from being able to budget, manage projects, and apply the same kind of systematic approach to Lean Sigma in order to achieve the excellent results seen in a corporate setting.

PI as a strategy in law firms
Clifford Chance

Some firms have made process improvement a cornerstone of their strategic endeavors. One firm that has reported good success with this approach is Clifford Chance, a Magic Circle firm in the UK. Clifford Chance has trained all of its lawyers in continuous improvement.

In January 2014, the firm announced that it had published a white paper on the use of continuous improvement stating that: "Clifford Chance is at the forefront of the deployment of Continuous Improvement techniques in the legal sector".[2] The paper discusses the firm's "experiences over the past five years of applying this methodology within an elite law firm; the benefits experienced by our clients and by the firm; and our views on how Continuous Improvement will be used by lawyers in the future."

The firm highlights case studies on the use of Lean Six Sigma at Clifford Chance, including document review flow in litigation. They report: "We were able to increase the flow of documents through the review team – which comprised both paralegals and junior lawyers – by giving them more efficient access to the experienced lawyers working on the matter. Queries from the review team were dealt with on a daily basis, therefore reducing the number of documents tagged incorrectly.

Feedback is immediate, giving the reviewers a clearer understanding of the documents and related issues. The introduction of a statistical 'sample size calculator' also enabled the team to decide, on a mathematical basis, the optimum number of documents to be checked for quality assurance purposes."

A second process improvement case study focuses on how the firm has made producing bound volumes easier, cheaper, and faster in transactions: "The new process has reduced the cost of producing a bound volume by approximately 60% and has reduced the time taken to dispatch a bound volume following the end of a transaction by up to 80%."

Another discusses how the firm has changed the way the client operates: "It is easy for private practice lawyers to believe that inefficiencies are inherent to a transaction, because the process is believed to reflect client needs. This was the case when we started a project reviewing a particular type of asset disposal we work on regularly for one of our clients. During the analysis, we identified a number of opportunities for improvement, including some changes that the client needed to make. We took our analysis and recommendations to the client and they were amenable to the proposed changes, including a suggestion that a different team at their end should be involved in some aspects of the transaction. Having implemented changes on both sides, these asset disposals are much smoother – and cheaper – for everyone involved."

Faegre Baker Daniels

Another example of a firm-wide approach to Lean Sigma can be found at Faegre Baker Daniels. Tom Snavely serves as manager of legal process improvement and project management for this AmLaw 100 firm with approximately 750 Lawyers in 14 offices across the US, UK, and China. According to Snavely, the firm has applied legal process improvement (LPI) and legal project management (LPM) to address the expanded use of alternative fee arrangements (AFAs), and the increased emphasis clients are placing on efficiency and value.

Faegre Baker Daniels has drawn a clear distinction between LPI and LPM and employed them in that sequence, using both top-down (i.e. efficiency is strategically important to the firm) and bottom-up (i.e. efficiency is important to my client/practice) approaches to promote internal adoption. This has allowed the firm to make great strides and achieve significant milestones in recent years.

In 2009, a legal process improvement/legal project management working group was formed at legacy firm Faegre & Benson. It included cross-functional operational executives. The first 30 professionals achieved Legal Lean Sigma® certification through the Legal Lean Sigma Institute (currently, there are more than 130 individuals trained firm-wide). The following year, the firm achieved early Legal Lean Sigma successes with real estate, eminent domain, and immigration projects. It also formed a Legal Process Improvement Community. By 2011, process improvement was included as a key topic at a firm partner retreat.

In 2012, the firm applied Legal Lean Sigma tools for post-combination integration work. The employment litigation and government advocacy and consulting groups also implemented project management tools. More recently, in 2013, Faegre Baker Daniels hosted efficiency-focused continuing legal education (CLE) from the firm's South Bend office. Process improvement projects were led by an even broader population from the internal LPI community.

As of 2014, Faegre Baker Daniels has actively applied LPI/LPM tools and methods in a variety of areas, including employment litigation (single-plaintiff claims defense), charitable solicitation registration for nonprofit organizations, various corporate filings, electronic court filings, immigration visa applications, time entry/client billing, and a joint LPI/LPM project for one of the firm's largest litigation clients. As internal and external demand for these services continues to grow, the number of legal services and administrative functions touched by process improvement at Faegre Baker Daniels is sure to expand.

Barley Snyder

Another example of a firm-wide initiative is that of Barley Snyder, which launched their Practice Excellence® program focused on quality, knowledge, and service in 2010. The mission of the program was to create a firm-wide and pervasive program of continuous improvement.

"Barley Snyder has made much progress in the past few years using internal resources and knowledge, but it was time to take Practice Excellence® to the next level," said Tim Dietrich, managing partner of the firm. Dietrich continued: "One method that [the firm used is] Lean Six Sigma, a recognized business strategy for increasing efficiency, identifying and eliminating obstacles, lowering costs, and improving the quality of the product or service."

Elliott Greenleaf

Another firm that has taken a systematic approach is Elliott Greenleaf, a 50-lawyer, full-service law firm in Delaware and Pennsylvania.

Impressively, this firm produced "13 Green Belts for a firm with fewer than 90 employees, or approximately 15 percent of the firm". The firm is not shy to point out that "By comparison, [another pioneering] firm has 75 Green Belts and one Black Belt among its 1,500 employees, only 5 percent."

"'We were excited about learning the Six Sigma language and skills,' says Neil Lapinski, shareholder. 'We not only can talk the talk everywhere that business people gather, we can now walk the walk.'"[3]

Seyfarth Shaw
Perhaps the best known firm to go to market in a big way with a firm-wide initiative, by 2009 Seyfarth Shaw had completed more than 75 projects, branded "SeyfarthLean", and reported that "[t]otal fees on certain legal projects reengineered through Six Sigma have been reduced from 13 percent to up to 50 percent".[4]

More recently, the firm reports that "More than five years ago, Seyfarth Shaw set out to see if there was a better way to drive value for our clients than the traditional model of delivering legal services. What we heard from our clients was the same then as it is now – a need for the efficient delivery of legal services, lower costs, budget predictability, quality work and value for fees. Urged by clients who had successfully implemented Six Sigma and Lean Six Sigma in their organizations, we invested in the approach to see if it might help us better meet our clients' needs.

The solution developed by Seyfarth was to work with experts to create a tailored version of Lean Six Sigma that could be implemented without the challenges presented by the strict Six Sigma and Lean approaches. We chose what we believe was best from both approaches for the legal industry and applied them to how we deliver legal services. Improved collaboration, communication, and efficiency are key objectives in adopting the process-driven methodologies that constitute this approach. With SeyfarthLean, we continually strive to perfect how we work with our clients and every day find new ways to improve the way we provide services."[5]

Berwin Leighton Paisner
Berwin Leighton Paisner used a systematic approach to develop sourcing capabilities that allowed them to develop their branded Integrated Client Services Model. "Berwin Leighton Paisner's Managed Legal Services (MLS) division brokered a deal with Thames Water in 2010 to run its own in-house legal team. The transaction is intended to give BLP greater

access to Thames Water's business and more opportunities for legal instructions.

MLS runs day-to-day legal matters for the company and refers work to Pannone in Manchester, South West firm Ashfords, as well as BLP itself.

Andrew MacNaughton, head of MLS, says that the business model allows general counsels to have a more strategic role in their organisation as well as making the in-house team cheaper to run. 'In terms of your in-house legal function, we can take that burden away and achieve a reduction of up to 20 percent or more on your annual legal spend,' he explains.

MacNaughton explains that in-house legal departments are rarely considered to be central to a company's business and could quite easily be outsourced to an organisation that has the processes and technology to run these teams more effectively. 'Less than 1% of companies have an internal legal support and most of them still succeed without the infrastructure and support,' he says. 'They go for legal advice as and when they need it. They just need an agile and nimble legal function that doesn't slow them down.'

MLS has two Lean Six Sigma practitioners within its ranks that focus on developing processes that create greater efficiency, consistency and certainty. In light of the Legal Services Act, MLS is looking for external investment as BLP under its partnership structure is not cash rich. The organisation is also likely to change its name and look for a shared services centre outside of London.

MacNaughton says that rate of change in the legal market is poised to significantly quicken: 'The landscape will be different. There will be lots of solutions to address the same problem and we will be one of them and it won't be centred around London.'"[6]

Just one year later, in March 2014, BLP announced its intention to launch a new integrated client services model. The firm indicated that legal process improvement services would be one of four key elements, along with virtual transaction teams, the use of third party providers, and a team in a new location that allowed the firm to offer client access to a "unique range of integrated services".

BLP stated that "The in-house LPI team has been deploying unique processes developed by BLP that have been applied to more than 60 work flows on existing client work streams. The LPI team is now expanding to provide more consultancy services for clients helping them to improve processes and analyse which balance of the options within the Integrated Service Model best addresses their needs."[7]

Valorem

In her 2012 article, "5 Firms Take Bold Approaches", part of a series of four related articles that appeared in the ABA *Law Practice* magazine, Susan Saltonstall Duncan reported on firms that made a decision to do things differently from the very start.[8]

In her interview with Patrick J. Lamb of Valorem Law Group, which is widely regarded as a firm that has led the "new normal" movement, Duncan reported:

"In 2008, when Patrick Lamb and three partners thought about starting a new kind of law firm focused on clients and value, they knew that a critical framework would be in pricing their services in a radically different way than their predecessor BigLaw firms (and most law firms) did. When they started setting fixed prices for their trial and litigation services, they realized that they needed to focus on the cost of providing those services – or they would never be profitable. Things would now have to be done faster, more efficiently and better than before."

One of the cornerstones of Valorem's business model is that project management and process improvement are essential. Duncan elaborated: "From the outset, lawyers took typical cases and produced process maps to delineate each step in the process. For example, before lawyers start to do any discovery on a case, they talk to the client first to establish an approach that is consistent with the client's desired outcome. The focus is on a full case assessment first, which dictates the fee, but more importantly, the value proposition and the winning strategy. The Valorem Toolbox provides tools for trial, budgeting, fee estimating and decision trees.

Client David Graham of DSW explains the process: 'First we sit down and discuss the business case and objective. At every turn, we determine whether and how an approach would deliver value to the business. Throughout the three years up to trial on a recent case, at each juncture we wrote down all the tasks and pieces that would be involved in the next chunk of work, evaluated the objectives, then priced it accordingly.'"

Larger ships are more difficult and take longer to change direction. But there is plenty of evidence that making this sort of change is not just possible, it is critical.

asb law

In May 2014, asb law announced the hire of a director of client services, Bernard Lazar, "with the specific remit of developing new and alternative offerings to clients adopting Lean service delivery methods and project management techniques underpinned by innovative technology that will support the new operational infrastructure".

According to the firm: "The appointment is a significant step in the restructuring of our business – a process which has been under way since late 2013. In a market-leading move, we have aligned our operations firmly to client needs by appointing partners to roles that reflect client businesses and not to usual legal disciplines. In his role, Lazar will work closely with partners in not only creating new propositions for clients, but in re-engineering the way in which legal services are delivered."

Commenting on the changes, managing partner Andrew Clinton explains: "For a number of years, clients of legal services have been requesting change from their external legal advisers – asking for more transparency, efficient and flexible resourcing of matters, and requesting a clear sense of certainty on budgets. By realigning our business to client segments, and by investing heavily in re-engineering our processes, we are responding to those requests. Bernard's experience in business transformation utilizing techniques such as process re-engineering, lean service delivery, six sigma and other project management tools will help us to deliver additional value to our clients."

Wilson Elser

Thus, there are some firms that are combining legal and business processes and applying both process improvement and project management to them. Peter Hitson, director of legal process innovation at Wilson Elser Moskowitz Edelman & Dicker LLP, explains that the firm's legal process innovation work is seen as a natural evolution of their focus on customers and their need for both effective and efficient legal services.

Founded in 1978, Wilson Elser has grown to nearly 800 lawyers in 26 offices across the US, one in London, and European affiliates. It is a full-service law firm with significant litigation experience and focus. Hitson says that "Wilson Elser includes Legal Project Management (LPM) and Legal Process Improvement (LPI) as part of its long-term vision and formal strategy. We have a rich base of existing processes, strong technology and practice groups aligned around key practice areas that help to share capabilities beyond our regional offices. What we wanted was greater uniformity in applying LPM and LPI as a core competency."

At this point, Hitson reports that the firm is "setting a vision and a road map for where we want to go over the next couple of years. The initiative matches our values and overall mission. Buy-in and leadership comes from the top. We are also building awareness and knowledge; about 100 lawyers from the chairman of the firm to associates have already participated in day-long training sessions. The firm is building on existing strengths and capabilities, engaging clients, and focusing on projects with particular clients and practice groups."

Wilson Elser, Hitson says, is "enjoying the flexibility to use a blend of project management and process improvement techniques and approaches. In terms of what's next, it's probably technology. A combination of increased client interest in collaborative budgeting and that link with LPM will have us both making sure we are fully using our existing capabilities and scanning the market for emerging solutions."

Designing a systematic change program

In a January 2007 article in the *Harvard Business Review*, author and former Konosuke Matsushita Professor of Leadership at Harvard Business School, John P. Kotter, points out that "[In] the more successful cases... the change process goes through a series of phases that, in total, usually require a considerable length of time. Skipping steps creates only the illusion of speed and never produces a satisfying result."[9]

In our steering committee workshops, we work with firms to design systematic change programs that guide a firm along the continuum from opportunistic to systematic improvements, where processes are stabilized, and scalable, and more connected and the firm achieves key performance measures relevant to key objectives. Our objectives behind a systematic change program include comprehensively redesigning the processes of a business to make them as capable and efficient as possible and to transform the performance of the business, and building the capacity for ongoing change.

The objectives of this kind of systematic approach are eventually to transform culture and the way the entire firm carries out its work, and to build lasting competitive advantage through processes that deliver the maximum value in high-quality legal services to clients at the lowest cost. To take this approach, the firm must believe that improvement is required (i.e. there is a compelling case for change) and must understand what improvements are needed and why. Furthermore, the goals for the change must be clear and credible; in other words, we must have measurable targets.

By taking a systematic approach, working with the DMAIC framework, following the process of process improvement, managing each process improvement project, and eventually building a culture of continuous improvement, law firms can create a "win-win-win" for business management, the legal department, and outside counsel.

Understanding corporate budgeting and the importance of predictability is of key importance. The financial links between excellent processes that are managed well – regardless of billing method – and profitability suggest that it is critical to take an approach that spans across an entire law firm in order to achieve the win-win-win.

References

1. Ryan, J., "Making the Case for Economic Quality, a White Paper for The American Society for Quality (ASQ)"; see http://asq.org/economic-case.
2. Clifford Chance, "Applying Continuous Improvement to high-end legal services"; whitepaper available at www.cliffordchance.com/content/dam/cliffordchance/About_us/Continuous_Improvement_White_Paper.pdf.
3. Law Firm Adopts Lean Strategy by the Delaware Manufacturing Extension Partnership.
4. Legal Biz Dev, "ACC Value Challenge (Part 2): Six Sigma at Seyfarth", 10 December 2008; see http://adverselling.typepad.com/how_law_firms_sell/2008/12/acc-value-challenge-part-2-six-sigma-at-seyfarth.html.
5. See www.seyfarth.com/seyfarthlean-background.
6. Crow, C., "Berwin Leighton Paisner's insourcing division", *The Know List* report, Issue 07, March 2013; see www.theknowlist.com/i7/index.html#/24.
7. Ibid.
8. Duncan, S. S., "5 Firms Take Bold Approaches" ABA Law Practice magazine, volume 38, No. 6, November/December 2012; see www.americanbar.org/publications/law_practice_magazine/2012/november-december/5-firms-take-bold-approaches.html.
9. Kotter, J.P., "Leading Change: Why Transformation Efforts Fail", Harvard Business Review, January 2007; see http://hbr.org/2007/01/leading-change-why-transformation-efforts-fail/ar/1.

Chapter 5:
Opportunistic approaches to employing Lean Six Sigma

While a systematic approach might be the most impactful, and the long term results it can produce the most desirable, the reality is that most firms begin by employing Lean Six Sigma opportunistically, taking advantage of pockets of interest and improving skills and discrete processes. This results in opportunistic improvements that are valuable but uneven across the organization and not always flowing to the bottom line.

Typically, opportunistic approaches occur because one person, usually a leader in a particular practice area or business function, determines that process improvement is worth trying. The most effective approach, in our experience, came from Morgan Lewis' eData Group, which recently invited clients to a two-day course and earned Yellow Belt certifications by learning, and working on, the processes of greatest interest to them (see Chapter 9).

With ever more legal services being deemed "commodity" type work, and the use of fixed fees and value-based billing increasing, we know that there is increasing pressure for firms to be highly efficient. Even with an opportunistic approach, the chances for differentiation and developing signature approaches are significant – and firms that are using process improvement to seize these opportunities are reaping the rewards.

Morgan Lewis applies Six Sigma to loan services – since 1974

Applying process improvement to a specific service that is viewed as commodity work is not new. Morgan Lewis, for example, was at the forefront with Six Sigma in application to its mortgage loan services. According to a case study by Richard J. Sabat, Six Sigma Green Belt at Morgan Lewis, the firm began applying Six Sigma to its loan services starting in 1974. This was first employed institutionally in 1988 with FDIC/RTC, retooled in 1997 with Total Quality Management, and then again with Six Sigma in 2000/2003. This is one of the earliest and most specific case studies I could find when I began to build the first of the

Legal Lean Sigma Institute's programs and certification courses (and then again in researching for and writing this report).

Sabat's case study provides excellent data on the approach used and the results achieved, including the fact that the firm was able to realize up to a 25 percent reduction in time charges and dramatically enhanced quality in mortgage loan services. While this type of reduction might not have been the most desirable result for a firm charging by the hour, it certainly is appealing to any client who is looking for the best, lowest cost solution, and to any firm performing the work for a fixed or capped fee.

Causes of defects (which is considered waste in Lean terms) were identified as: transaction data input, intermittent data flow, inefficient data communication to entire team, no data quality control, lack of standard forms, and poor quality forms (the precedent documents contained defects and there was a lack of baseline and/or quality control). Additionally, the Socratic associate training method employed by the firm reportedly resulted in a lack of written transaction practices and written standard operating procedures. Finally, time pressure and disorganization were also identified as causes.

Using the data gathered in the measure phase of the DMAIC framework, and the work performed in the analyze phase, Morgan Lewis developed their improvement ideas, which included human behavior items such as client protocols and standard practices and procedures. They also focused on what Sabat refers to as the "physics of the transaction", meaning data input and integrity, standard forms, and standard communication. Interestingly, document preparation software was part of their solution.

The charts included in the case study show very compelling "before", "early Six Sigma", and "later Six Sigma" graphical results, indicating that the firm did not just improve the process once; they committed to continuous improvement and realized better results each time they improved how they performed and delivered work in this area.

Combining process improvement and project management at Fisher Matthews PLLC

One of the best examples of a service that realized extraordinary benefits from combining process improvement and project management comes from commercial real estate attorney Rebekah Fisher. Fisher, currently of Fisher Matthews PLLC, formerly of Waller Lansden Dortch and Davis, Dinsmore & Shohl LLP, developed an excellent process to prepare, negotiate, and execute a great number of commercial leases each year for a large retailer client. She improved her commercial real estate practice in a way that resulted in the highest levels of client satisfaction and excellent profitability for her practice and firm.

In order to perform this work profitably using an alternative fee structure for the portfolio of work, Fisher focused on standardizing her process, communications, forms, and leases. She explained that she uses only very organized and efficient timekeepers, which involves staffing with the lowest-cost resources capable of doing each activity. Detailed data about the effort it takes to both do and deliver this work is kept, which allowed Fisher to continually refine her model process and very effectively manage the work and resources.

The results are impressive. Fisher reports that they improved their response time from the receipt of the client's request to producing a draft of lease to either the same or the next day. They also reduced the overall time it takes from their receipt of the client's request to the execution of a lease from 168 days to 62 days.

It is important to translate improvements into benefits: Fisher's fast, reliable results have allowed the client to open stores an average of eight weeks earlier that was previously possible. This is worth tens of millions of dollars in increased revenue for their client. Thus, in addition to the fact that this process allows the law firm to deliver this service profitably and reliably for a low fixed fee, their client's high satisfaction with the results has them singing Fisher's praises. This, in turn, has resulted in new, referred business for the firm.

OFCCP audit process improvement at Ogletree, Deakins, Nash, Smoak & Stewart, PC

An improved OFCCP audit process was one of the many projects tackled at Ogletree, Deakins, Nash, Smoak & Stewart, PC. This project was championed by practice group leader Leigh Nason, whose practice includes representing federal contractors and sub-contractors in compliance evaluations and administrative enforcement actions triggered by the United States Department of Labor's Office of Federal Contract Compliance Programs (OFCCP).

The project team included lawyers, paralegals, knowledge management professionals, and data analysts. The goals of the project were to create a consistent, branded process for AAP preparation, OFCCP audit defense, and various other services such as EEO-1 reporting, compliance assessments, etc. – anything in the group's area of service that would benefit from a consistent workflow process – define the lowest cost timekeeper capable of doing a task and ensure that appropriate work is funneled to those people, promote the new process internally (to their referrers) and externally (to new and existing clients), and ensure that all practice group members are "on board" with the new process.

Additionally, Nason wanted to train and generate awareness among other practice group members and referrers within the firm as to what the service was and how the work was performed. Furthermore, she knew that it was important to "ensure a basic level of competence among all attorneys and specialized knowledge of various areas (such as applicant/hire analysis, testing, etc.) among a few attorneys. The improved process had to facilitate the ability to generate a specific dollar amount (number intentionally omitted) in additional revenue and we had to be able to measure that revenue with some degree of certainty."

Moreover, the project goals included an increase in practice group services-related billings of each timekeeper (other than the top generator) by at least 10 percent. Underlying this idea was the need to create such a good process that Nason, the practice group leader, could manage a "virtual" practice group of attorneys, analysts, and staff in various offices.

After measuring and analyzing many aspects of the process, the team drew inspiration from great coaches and sports teams to develop creative improvements and solutions. Examples included developing a "playbook" with a current roster/directory, and specific "plays" (checklists, forms, etc.) so that quality assurance and consistency is guaranteed, regardless of the client or attorney working on the project. The team also clarified guidelines regarding credits, opening matters, and rates and also ensured that the premium rates for this niche practice work were not "watered down" by insurance rates.

As is the case with many (even most, if not all) process improvement projects, and in keeping with the project goals, the team identified specific training and professional development needs for the group, including business analysts. "An effective communication strategy and specific procedures for working with referrers that included checkpoints, exchanging client development information and otherwise ensuring that we continue to keep referrers "in the loop" with regard to clients entrusted to us were developed and implemented. Additionally, standardized communications were established for consistency in messaging within the practice area and the firm. This includes simple but critical items such as file naming conventions across the practice area team and organizing data files in a highly specified file structure on a shared drive with standardized file names and email subjects. The new process also ensures that relevant information is stored on the firm's document management system and on a dedicated drive for practice group matters", says Nason.

The team also developed new practice group codes to better identify various components of practice area in order to measure profit, utilization, growth trends, and contractions. Another outcome of the project was established standard operating procedure of formalizing the relationship with the client on new matters, e.g. use of specific language (on documents such as engagement letters) to clarify details and logistics.

Following the project, the practice group took additional actions based on the team's recommendations. They engaged in strategic planning, where they developed core values and a mission statement to ensure that the team had a common purpose and was going in the same direction. Later, the practice group organized and conducted a two-day "boot camp" for all practice group members (attorneys, non-attorneys, administrator, and coordinator) to increase knowledge and train on the new processes.

The project also led them to establish a practice group administrator and coordinator. The administrator works directly with Nason as the practice group head on administrative matters, assigns analysts to prepare AAPs, monitors workflow and timeliness of AAP and audit preparation, interfaces with clients to respond to questions or triage them to attorneys, and serves as final quality control. The coordinator has assumed marketing and client service responsibilities that formerly were handled by the firm's client services group. This ensures that the practice group has a person with an intimate knowledge of their practice group services who is staffing exhibit booths and talking with clients (and potential clients) at conferences and seminars. The coordinator also sources various seminars for speaking opportunities. She is also responsible for quality control for AAP preparation. Both the practice group administrator and the coordinator are also timekeepers who bill hours.

This project delivered important results: the practice group's fixed-fee AAPs are profitable; and they know which fixed fee arrangements are the most and least profitable. Also, OFCCP work is now delivered even more profitably and by an expanded team. Overall, they have increased the number of new matters over previous years, increased their billings and hours, and have robust and successful marketing.

Team member T. Scott Kelly, a shareholder who is also an active member of the American Bar Association's Section of Labor and

Employment Law (where he currently is the employer co-chair of the Section's marketing committee), reflects on the OFCCP audit process improvement project his team delivered: "We initially sought to improve the manner in which we performed and delivered services to our clients. Our new process has increased our internal efficiencies, which we are able to pass along to our clients. These efficiencies are not confined to competitive pricing, which is a benefit, but also include precise and thoughtful client interactions."

Kelly goes on to point out, "Additionally, the Kaizen identified specific improvements to the interactions with lawyers in our firm that referred us work. Focusing on the manner, the content, and the amount of information we communicate with them has raised the referrers' level of satisfaction with our practice group. Another plus is the standardization of this process reduces the time involved in the process. So, we are keeping our clients and internal referrers happier, providing them more information, but with no loss to our own efficiencies."

Process improvement in litigation

Litigation is often an area in which it is initially more difficult to imagine how process improvement can be helpful. Two case studies that were published by Lisa Damon of Seyfarth Shaw in January 2014 are instructive in this regard.[1]

The first case study involved a retailer facing an increased number of personal injury lawsuits relating to store conditions: "In each case, the plaintiff alleged unique facts that led to the injury. However, across the lawsuits, the facts about the stores were relatively consistent. Each lawsuit was covered by insurance if the costs to defend plus damages or settlement exceeded $250,000, but almost no cases were resolved above that threshold.

At the inception of the process improvement program, the retailer faced more than 100 lawsuits, with an average cost per lawsuit of approximately $50,000. A combination of process improvement and project management, with the use of an AFA, helped the retailer manage its defense costs. In particular: Although the plaintiff's facts varied by lawsuit, the steps to defend were comparable. This allowed the legal team to consolidate tasks and develop a consistent approach. Through the AFA, the retailer achieved predictability for defense costs and incentivized outside counsel to increase efficiency in its practices. The integrated approach reduced the volume of lawsuits pending in the portfolio from approximately 100 at any given time to less than 10. The average cost per lawsuit also dropped from approximately $50,000 to less than $10,000. Overall, the retailer lowered its projected uninsured risk exposure from $5 million to $100,000."

The second case study included in Damon's article involved managing a litigation portfolio: "A large US defense contractor with multiple business units across the country needed a single law firm to handle its high volume of litigation and counseling needs. The client identified greater consistency in practices, quality of outcomes, and efficiency as success targets for the legal team.

Process improvement was key to meeting the client's objectives and delivering value. With input and support from the in-house lawyers, the selected law firm:

- Conducted extensive 'voice of the client' interviews with corporate and division counsel to identify issues and potential root causes at the portfolio and matter levels.

- Developed a standard trial process map to assess each case for its potential to go to trial on the front end and throughout the case.

- Launched a new trial approach that triaged cases and staffing based on potential risk, with a flat fee AFA.

The overall strategy led to improved outcomes and provided the client with greater predictability of its legal expenses. It created cost savings of 30% on an average per-matter basis for single-plaintiff employment litigation, based on a five-year track record of nearly 180 matters."

Increased efficiency and reduced errors at The Hunoval Firm

More recently, in March 2014, the *American Bar Association Journal* reported on The Hunoval Firm in North Carolina. This foreclosure firm believes in investing in deep skill development "by sending staff to training based on real projects being developed for the firm" and expects "a full 70% to be trained by the end of 2014". The *ABA Journal* article also mentions that the firm's "first project addressed the overly long process for a notice of hearing and achieved the impressive 88% timeline improvement."[2]

The firm says it has saved an estimated $4 million since 2012 through increased efficiencies, better timelines, and error reduction. It has, for instance, reduced the time it takes to file a North Carolina notice of hearing (NOH) from an average of 70 days to around eight.

"I knew that we would attain real operational benefits – increased efficiencies and reduction in errors – and it would help us run a better, more efficient law firm management," says Hunoval.[3] But, he adds, there were also a lot of unexpected benefits including workforce engagement and marketing.

Lean Six Sigma for mergers and acquisitions at Husch Blackwell

In his whitepaper "An Unconventional Alliance: Lessons from a Lean Six Sigma Pilot",[4] Lann Wasson of Husch Blackwell LLP reflects that "A complex mergers and acquisitions practice is an unlikely place to start a Lean Six Sigma pilot in a large law firm. Conventional wisdom would suggest that these methodologies from the manufacturing sector would more likely fit the operational side of the firm, as well as the more repetitive matters in commoditized practice areas. So in April 2010, when the chair of Husch Blackwell's mergers and acquisitions practice invited me to participate in a pilot to assist lawyers in using Lean Six Sigma on acquisitions, I knew that there would be many hours of work and challenges ahead for the whole team.

The genesis of the pilot started months earlier as lawyers in the firm began investigating different approaches to matter management, alternative fee pricing and a greater degree of leverage. While it was tempting to simply fine-tune existing approaches in an effort to control costs, these lawyers recognized that a new approach was needed to address the root causes of deal expense and client frustration. By identifying ways to achieve client goals more efficiently and effectively, the partners aimed to differentiate their services to ultimately give their clients a marketplace advantage and the firm greater market share.

Of the range of project management and process improvement methods available, the chair selected Lean Six Sigma as the pilot's frame of reference because these methodologies resonated with a cross section of the business community, including success in service sectors such as health care and banking. Furthermore, the tenets of Lean and Six Sigma, such as listening to clients, continuous improvement, process thinking and measurement, distinguished these approaches from others commonly used within the legal industry and promised to challenge status quo assumptions. Since the partners worked with different types of clients – from private equity investors to strategic buyers – the team needed an approach like Lean Six Sigma, which would allow them to develop their capability to collaborate with a client to design a framework that could improve its approach to deal management."

Capturing firm experience at Pillsbury

Opportunistically improving business processes can deliver excellent results as well. Kathleen T. Pearson is director of administration for Pillsbury's global operations center in Nashville, TN. The center houses the firm's global operations staff, including IT, human resources, document production, finance, and accounting, as well as significant portions of the marketing department. Kathleen is responsible for managing all day-to-day functions of the 150+ person office and coordinating operational needs for attorneys throughout the firm's 14 other locations. A Six Sigma Green Belt, Legal Lean Sigma Yellow Belt, and graduate of George Washington University's Master's in Law Firm Management, Pearson is helping Pillsbury to achieve better efficiencies in firm operations.

While at Waller Lansden, Pearson delivered a process improvement project to capture firm experience that had a significant impact on operations and the firm's ability to understand and discuss its relevant experience with clients, prospects and referrers. The problem statement for the project was that the firm was not capturing its firm experience efficiently. Says Pearson, "Not having this information resulted in having to initiate a fire drill every time we needed specific experience for a proposal or client meeting; we ultimately were submitting incomplete information."

Her project included mapping the process in detail, which allowed her to identify specific issues and explore alternative "process designs" that eliminated waste and rework and educated employees. One improvement was that the firm created a useful tool in the form of a new data input screen. The result speaks for itself: the firm saw an improved capture of firm experience from 6 percent to 100 percent.

Combining opportunistic and systematic approaches

Since opportunistic approaches can dramatically differ, the examples can be found in many places along the continuum. For example, Gimbal Canada Inc. presented its 2013 work in a presentation to law students at the University of Ottawa in January 2014,[5] reporting that "Borden Ladner Gervais has mapped 30 processes (from litigation to M&A) and now uses its maps for training, KM and marketing." A different kind of success story included in the same presentation references a Virginia firm that "saved 30 hours and $21,000 by reducing set-up time in one afternoon, in the very first process they looked at".

Thompson Hine reports that it employs a combination of systematic and opportunistic approaches. The firm has invested heavily in resources, structure, and "air time", preaching the gospel of legal project management, process improvement, value billing, and staffing. The firm has dedicated resources, including its director of legal project management; its manager of pricing; working groups established to assist in successfully scoping, launching, managing and closing matters; and software, some of which was created by the firm, to model and optimize staffing, project milestones, budget, and actual spending, among other hard assets that have to be in place to truly succeed in integrating the rigors of matter management and efficiency in work. The firm is passionate about ingraining this approach firm-wide.

Acknowledging that vision doesn't come overnight, they couple the firm-wide effort with targeted opportunistic work. "Some matters present perfect circumstances for LPM, knowledge management tools, and alternative approaches to staffing. They are prime examples that can be held out for our lawyers to see the benefits of project management. Clients endorse these tools and love the results. The lawyers need to get on this bus," says Deborah Read, managing partner of Thompson Hine.

Thompson Hine notes five critical factors a firm needs to have in place to be successful as an opportunist:

1. Data – in the right form and accessible to the right people managing the matter;

2. An administrative team with the knowledge and bandwidth to create and support the legal team;

3. Basic tools to create the roadmap (client dialogue, scope, work plan, reporting, ongoing dialogue);

4. Impetus – whether internally derived or externally through the specifics of the engagement; and

5. A motivated partner who wants to lead with this approach.

Further, Thompson Hine outlines how those five critical success factors differ in order to be successful systematically across the firm:

1. Data – still an imperative, but the firm has to truly master the data;

2. Administrative team with the knowledge and bandwidth to create and support the legal team and an understanding of how tools and processes may need to be adapted to fit differing practices;

3. More sophisticated tools deployed firm-wide – technology underpinnings, collaboration tools, financial tools to model staffing and project management plans along with corresponding budget, ability to track spending, staffing deployment, matter project vs. budget, etc.;

4. Demonstrated reward for applying the approach – internal or external; and

5. Firm culture shift.

Everywhere in a law firm, there are processes that range from simple to complicated but all can be improved. Thomas L. Sager and Scott L. Winkelman, make the following recommendations:

- "Start with paper processes, which often lend themselves to standardized process improvements, and often yield quick victories.

- Map the process – mundane though it sounds, mapping often yields dramatic results by highlighting the process as it really exists

- Target unconscious spending – staff often take action without even considering the costs

- Apply information technology – IT fixes often bubble up early

- Leverage the learning – multiply the benefits by leveraging project learning to similar processes and functions

- Be a forum for pent-up grievances – pent-up pet peeves are often the stuff of superb process improvement projects."[6]

The sequences and principles of Lean and Six Sigma are straightforward and clear. The logic of DMAIC, both in concept and application, begins to make more and more sense as law firms try to make their processes more efficient. There are many ways to select a first project but, if in doubt, your clients' feedback is an excellent place to get ideas about where to start.

References

1. Damon, L., "Applying Lean Six Sigma Methods to Litigation Practice" (practice note), *Practical Law*, January 2014; see http://us.practicallaw.com/9-549-6388?q=&qp=&qo=&qe=.

2. Carter, T., "Foreclosure firm goes statistical to improve speed and quality",

American Bar Association Journal online; www.abajournal.com/magazine/article/foreclosure_firm_goes_statistical_to_improve_speed_and_quality.

3. PEX, "CEO of Hunoval Law Firm: Lean Six Sigma was a 'lighbulb moment'"; see www.processexcellencenetwork.com/lean-six-sigma-business-transformation/articles/six-sigma-in-law-interview-with-matt-hunoval.

4. Wasson, L., "An Unconventional Alliance: Lessons from a Lean Six Sigma Pilot", ILTA white paper, June 2011; see www.huschblackwell.com/~/media/Files/BusinessInsights/BusinessInsights/2011/06/ILTA%20White%20Paper%20An%20Unconventional%20Alliance%20Less__/Files/An%20Unconventional%20Alliance%20Lessons%20from%20a%20Lean%20S__/FileAttachment/WassonILTA2011.pdf.

5. See http://gimbalcanada.com/professional-development.

6. Sager T.L., and Winkelman, S.L., "Six Sigma: Positioning for Competitive Advantage", ACCA Docket 19, No. 1, 2001.

Chapter 6:
Closest to the pin and efficiency – Thriving when legal procurement is in the mix

By Dr Silvia Hodges Silverstein, vice president, strategic market development of Sky Analytics

The involvement of procurement in the purchasing of legal services is one of the side effects of a power shift to the client. The siren song to law firms is get your cost house in order, improve your efficiency and processes, sharpen your pencil, and come out ready for the new world of legal procurement.

Unless you sit across from corporate purchasing, procurement, sourcing, or supply managers in a pitch, they are the anonymous people accused of everything from interfering with the lawyer-client relationship, having neither the knowledge nor ability to judge the quality of legal services, playing firms against each other and cherry-picking in order to get the lowest price, and unreasonably squeezing firms' margins. With the help of procurement, more and more companies have been taking a more rigorous approach to selecting firms and ensuring that the relationship continues to deliver expected outcomes. Corporate purchasing has changed the way professional services are bought over the last few decades: engineering and architectural services since the late 1980s; marketing, public relations, and advertising services since the mid-late 1990s; accounting, auditing, and tax services since the early- to mid-2000s; and legal services in the last five plus years.

Legal budgets are under cost scrutiny like any other part of an organization, since legal spend has become a significant line item that no CEO or CFO can ignore. Top management sees legal departments as cost centers and wants legal to be managed efficiently and effectively. They call on procurement to get the job done: spending less on suppliers can directly improve the bottom line. Procurement's mandate is traditionally based on the idea of cost control, getting external suppliers to reduce their prices, and preventing departments from unnecessary spending through managing what is purchased. Top management is very aware of the strategic benefits that can be achieved through the intelligent use of purchasing and supply management.

General counsel are no longer the only buyers of corporate legal services

Procurement takes a process-driven, business-to-business sourcing approach. This approach may collide with the traditional, relationship-driven selection by in-house counsel. Procurement adds process expertise and makes the selection more objective and transparent. Procurement professionals negotiate hard and facilitate the sourcing process. Procurement assists in-house lawyers with defining the scope of the project, selecting the right supplier, negotiating and structuring compensation, evaluating supplier performance, and leveraging business with preferred suppliers. Their involvement allows in-house lawyers to focus on what they do best – the world of law, rather than having to deal with selecting the right legal service providers. And with in-house counsel's pay increasingly tied to legal spend management and staying within budget, procurement is now more often embraced by in-house counsel than it once was.

How has procurement's role evolved in the last few years? I conducted three researches on legal procurement: my first study in 2011 in collaboration with the Institute for Supply Management and the American Purchasing Society, a second one in 2012, and a third in 2014. The majority of the respondents in these researches were from large companies, Fortune 500 and 1000 companies, and a smaller number were medium-sized companies.

Legal procurement continues to gain influence

Each research showed that procurement practices gained influence and achieved greater levels of savings. In 2011, sophisticated legal procurement was a minority skill at large companies. By 2014, we are seeing the bulk of the major buyers of legal services turn to procurement professionals to buy more for less. Large corporations employ their own legal procurement team and medium-sized companies hire consultants that organize legal procurement consortiums to achieve greater buying power. In 2012, half of the respondents influenced less than 20 percent of the legal budget. The number has grown to 28 percent today. On the upper end, in 2012, only a small number (less than 10 percent of respondents), claimed to influence "over 90 percent" or "all" of the legal budget. This number rose to 25 percent in 2014. Readers should note that a portion of legal spend may not be part of the legal budget, but owned by different business unit stakeholders.

The involvement of procurement typically starts with the negotiation of master service agreements (MSA), management of the panel selection, or legal commodities such as e-discovery. This is often done through so-called "reverse auctions". In a reverse auction, a client puts work out for bid, using specialized software or online. Multiple firms offer bids on the work and compete with each other to offer the lowest price that meets all of the specifications of the bid. Standard practices also include billing guidelines and a robust invoice review process, as well as case management guidelines. The intelligent use of purchasing helps companies rein in rising legal costs by separating legal services into commoditized segments, including paralegal and research needs, and creating sourcing strategies for individual segments.

Master negotiators and bad cops

Legal procurement's main role is that of a "buyer" and "influencer". As buyers, legal procurement professionals are responsible for price and contract negotiation, as well as for the engagement letter, retainer, or framework agreement. Legal and procurement often assume "good cop" and "bad cop" roles: as in-house counsel, if you have to deal with your counterparts every day, it is much better to have procurement people be the tough negotiators. It does not destroy in-house lawyers' working relationship with outside counsel. As influencers, they aim to affect the outcome of a decision with their opinion.

Another common role for legal procurement professionals is "gate-keeper": legal procurement professionals control the flow of information from the firm to the deciders. They are less likely to be "deciders" themselves; only rarely do they make the final decision regarding which firm to choose or have the ability to veto a decision that has been made.

The general counsel and their designated lawyers still retain the right to short-list firms. This has not changed. In some companies, senior executives, such as the CEO or the board, are also involved in short-listing law firms. Business management, such as division heads or business unit managers, appear to have less influence today on which firms are short-listed than procurement, compared to the 2012 study.

The general counsel, and to a lesser degree, other in-house lawyers, also have a final say in the selection of the company's legal service providers. CEOs and other management are typically not involved in the final decision. A CEO cares about the total cost and the win rate. They typically delegate specific choice to the general counsel. Legal procurement professionals are rarely the "initiators" of sourcing legal service. It is typically the in-house lawyers suggesting which legal services are needed.

In line with their roles, legal procurement professionals are most likely to be involved in the negotiation and contract development phase and in the development of (purchasing) criteria and strategy. Post-purchase evaluation of legal services providers has become an important part of their work. Legal procurement professionals are least likely to be involved in the selection phase of legal service providers. Despite the widely held belief among lawyers that procurement officers normally buy widgets and are ill equipped to understand and buy legal services, about one fifth of legal procurement professionals have a legal background. The remaining majority of respondents in the studies held MBA degrees or bachelor degrees in business-subjects.

From legal commodities to high-stakes work

Procurement is typically involved in purchasing routine services, but has made progress in purchasing "bread and butter" legal services, those between high-stakes work and commodities. According to the 2014 study, procurement is increasingly involved in the purchasing of complex, high-value, high-stakes legal services. GlaxoSmithKline is a pioneer in this area. The pharmaceutical giant uses a procurement approach to all legal matters in excess of $250,000.[1] GSK's general counsel, Dan Troy, says that involving procurement paid off; in the nearly four years since GlaxoSmithKline looked to revamp the way it hires and pays for outside legal services, the pharmaceutical giant has saved tens of millions of dollars in legal fees, according to a 2012 article in *The Legal Intelligencer.*[2]

The intelligent use of purchasing helps companies rein in rising legal costs by separating legal services into commoditized segments, including paralegal and research needs, and creating sourcing strategies for individual segments. Procurement is also involved in all types of legal services: litigation, transactional, and to a somewhat lesser degree, advisory work. It appears that no stones are left unturned. All types of matters have become subject to scrutiny.

Who pays sticker price?

Unless alternative fee arrangements are used, legal procurement professionals clearly expect discounts on law firm's rack rates, according to the 2014 study. "You would not buy sticker price at the car dealer", a legal procurement professional at a Fortune 100 company pointed out to me. But just how much of a discount do they expect?

- Half of the respondents in the study expect a discount of over 20 percent.
- What's more, about a quarter of respondents expect a discount of over 25 percent.

However, if so much importance is placed upon the hourly rate discounts, legal procurement professionals should also monitor what other metrics this impacts. In other words, if I negotiate a steep discount, will that affect the level of experience on a matter, where the work is done, or the staffing efficiency? It is important to embrace analytics and look at total cost and see a more holistic picture of legal spend, rather than just focusing on discounts.

Legal procurement analyzes many things that might not have been given a lot of attention in the legal profession before:

- Industry benchmarking analysis (conducted by 71 percent of respondents);
- Rate increase analysis and invoice audits (67 percent each);
- Half of the respondents forecast budgets, followed by alternative fee arrangement analysis, and key performance indicator analysis;
- Procurement also embraces legal spend management (75 percent) and e-billing (71 percent);
- Contract database for legal matter management and in-house e-discovery are used by 40–50 percent of respondents in the survey; and
- Firms' project management and process improvement capabilities are increasingly important: 48 percent of respondents in the survey deemed them "very important", another 16 percent as "important".

What are procurement's other tools? How do they manage to reach their goals? Billing guidelines are still the most common standard practices when sourcing legal services. 81 percent of respondents said they use them in their organization. It is good procurement practice to make the organization's terms and conditions (T&C) be part of the minimum requirements upfront. T&C should get accepted before a request for proposal (RFP) is issued, together with a non-disclosure agreement (NDA). Attempts to deviate from the T&C typically count against the firm during the evaluation process. Also important are invoice review processes (70 percent). Case management and counsel selection and evaluation processes as well as analysis have gained in importance since the 2012 survey.

RFPs: A tire-kicking exercise?

Many law firms are busy filling in requests for proposal (RFPs) issued or initiated by legal procurement. Is it worth their time? How often do new suppliers win business over the incumbent law firms in an RFP issued by their organization? "Sometimes", says the majority (58 percent) of legal procurement professionals. "Often" say 25 percent. "Rarely" say 17 percent. Nobody answered "All the time" or "Never".

Law firms are advised to have a clear understanding of whether an RFP is a tire-kicking exercise or if the company is looking for alternatives to their current firms. Law firms need to carefully qualify opportunities and be clear of their go/no-go criteria to avoid wasting their time and resources. A misguided service mentality of marketing and business development would be to help partners with every RFP that lands on their desks. Not every RFP should receive the same level of attention. The firm needs to have a clear understanding of when they draw the line or when an "opportunity" presented is not one that they should be interested in. Only RFPs that are in line with the firm's strategy should be pursued.

It is worth speaking directly with the client to learn more about how procurement works in their organization, what influence procurement has, and how the two departments collaborate. It is important to start building a relationship with the client's legal procurement. As a key stakeholder with growing influence, most procurement officers are open to learning more about what services firms currently provide and those the firm may be able to provide in the future. They may be looking for ways to consolidate spend, or to increase spend with the goal of getting volume discounts. Law firms should be aware of procurement's goals, objectives, challenges, and strategies.

Strategies for law firms

The involvement of procurement and their way of comparing law firms requires a different approach from the firms themselves; they need to consider a different way than just thinking in terms of hourly rates and billing. Procurement professionals demand predictability and project and budget management even more than most GCs. It is advisable to understand what the client values; in particular, which metrics the organization uses when evaluating law firms. More and more companies are data and metrics driven, conduct detailed cost analysis, and plan and manage their organizations with sophisticated metrics and benchmarks, which influences their selection.

The chief procurement officer (CPO) of a large company shared with me that "if you know your business, you should know how long something takes and how much something should cost". He used to work in the nuclear energy sector, which in his opinion had many more unpredictable factors and was much more complex than your average litigation. Yet, the engineers were able to come up with a price. He thought that lawyers being unable – or unwilling – to put a price tag on a piece of work told him that they did not really know their business. He assumed that lawyers never bothered to analyze their business, because they did not have to.

Generally speaking, legal procurement professionals look for experience with similar matters or "closest to the pin". Has the firm done similar work for another client? Argued in front of this judge or court? Solved a similar issue? Procurement wants to be sure the law firm will hit the ground running. Many might have the general expertise, but which firm will not need to do extensive, expensive research to get up to speed? It is good practice to ask firms to present examples or case studies to demonstrate the ways in which they have solved similar problems and how they work with clients and other law firms. Firms can also win points with procurement if they can show industry experience as it also promises the efficiency procurement seeks. Finally, value for money and service excellence are important factors for procurement. Procurement wants to see efficiency. A robust project management approach helps do just that.

For procurement, there are a number of subjective factors that influence the decision to award work to a particular law firm. According to the survey, the most important were:

- Responsiveness ("They are willing to help us to provide prompt service");
- Reliability ("They are able to perform the service dependably and

accurately");

- Availability ("They are there when we need them");
- Chemistry ("We like working with them");
- Empathy ("They make an effort to know our company and its needs"); and
- Assurance ("They have the required skills and knowledge to perform the service").

These subjective factors all ranked above previous relationships with specific lawyers. Contrast these with what lawyers typically place a lot of value on – peer recommendations and industry rankings – factors that have little importance for legal procurement professionals. The (lowest) price, which was one of the two least important factors in the 2012 study, on the other hand, has gained in importance. Clients appear to be less shy about their intent to save cost.

When assessing a firm's value-adds, legal procurement see great value in continued legal education (CLE) seminars and business-level training, as well as "hotline" access for quick questions or to discuss new matters. Other desired value-adds include: in-person visits to the client's office, plant, or facility to get to know their business; participation on internal calls that provide insight into a specific business or practice area; secondments; provision or development of basic templates and forms; conducting pre-matter planning sessions; and share-points with real-time access to the company's documents.

With legal procurement quickly growing in influence, law firms are advised to understand how procurement works and to collaborate with them. While procurement may not be the final decision-maker, the findings of all three legal procurement studies clearly suggest that firms are well advised to work with procurement, understand what is important to them, and to create a capability to respond to procurement demands. The time to invest in proposal preparation, project management and process improvement, analysis, and cost control is now.

The study was conducted in Q1 2014 by Dr Silvia Hodges Silverstein, vice president, strategic market development of Sky Analytics, and lecturer in law, Columbia Law School & adjunct professor, Fordham Law School. Links to the survey programmed on Qualtrics were posted to LinkedIn (legal) procurement groups and sent to a list of legal procurement professionals by email. 40 percent of respondents had the title procurement/purchasing/sourcing manager. 32 percent had the title chief procurement/purchasing officer or director of procurement/purchasing/sourcing. The majority of respondents came from Fortune 100 and Fortune 1000 companies. Most respondents said that their company had involved procurement in the sourcing of legal services for three or more years. Silvia Hodges Silverstein can be reached at silvia. hodges@skyanalytics.com or hodges@silviahodges.com.

References

1. See the recent case study I co-authored with Heidi K. Gardner for an in-depth look into the company's approach. Gardner, Heidi K., and Silverstein, S.H., "GlaxoSmithKline: Sourcing Complex Professional Services", Harvard Business School Case 414-003, September 2013. (Revised June 2014.)

2. Passarella, G., "GlaxoSmithKline Saves Millions in Legal Fees With Value-Based Programs", *The Legal Intelligencer*, 9 July 2012; see www.thelegalintelligencer.com/search-results-layout-page?query=dan+troy+glaxo&source=nylitnews%2Clawdecision&sort=date&direction=descending&start=1&end=10&returnType=json#ixzz38Jdr7X68.

Chapter 7:
Getting started and structuring for success

Other law firms and legal departments are using process improvement to their advantage. So, we can continue to operate as we always have and allow a performance gap to develop. Or we can take action.

We can:

- Seize the momentum that exists in the legal space to address the challenge of reconnecting value to costs for legal services, as espoused by the ACC Value Challenge;

- Determine the definition of value by considering different models, such as John Grant's value theory; and

- Greatly improve our ability to develop AFAs and value-based billing with a new model for looking at, improving, and managing work – and the way it is delivered.

My experience is that law firms will benefit enormously by building deep skills in improving processes and that the firms that do this soonest will accrue significant advantages. That said, it is true that developing the levels of skill and experience required to carry out process improvement projects efficiently and effectively is not a trivial matter and requires a significant investment of time and resources.

In a December 2012 blog post, Timothy B. Corcoran writes: "If you want to improve your law practice, your business, your customer service posture, then you need to ask two simple questions, and ask them regularly: *What are we doing well* and *what can we improve?*" Corcoran suggests that: "It's critical to know explicitly and specifically what clients value, why they value it, and that they want us to continue doing it."[1]

Corcoran goes on to state: "If you don't know *explicitly* what your clients value about your service and if you don't know *explicitly* what they wish you would do better, then all the charts and graphs and analysis are just so much statistical noise... [S]ustainable profitability comes from client satisfaction; client satisfaction comes from continuous improvement; continuous improvement happens when we regularly ask our clients what we do well and what we can improve. It's that simple… there is no better job security than channeling the voice of the customer, and this isn't hard to do."

Thus, some firms begin their process improvement initiative very simply. Others have investigated, considered, and then opt to begin with a conscious decision to make process improvement a cornerstone of their firm's strategic plan. Obviously, this is a radically different approach and a larger level of investment will be needed. Many firms may want to start out by "dipping their toes in the water", developing some skills first, and deciding later to dive into process improvement. The point is that there is no one right way to start.

All firms should understand and take into account the driving and restraining forces in their own organization that will either support a Lean Sigma project or initiative or work against it. More specifically, one of the biggest challenges to doing process improvement work in law firms lies in the lack of availability, accessibility, or quality of good data. This explains why some firms are undertaking projects related to improving their timekeeping processes.

Without reliable and complete data, it is difficult (if not impossible) to tell how much effort it takes to do and deliver any particular work. This impacts a firm's ability to make important business decisions, including those related to strategy, pricing, staffing, infrastructure, and more.

Timekeeping is a critical process

Because the data in law firms is often less than stellar, process improvement teams sometimes look to industry data, such as the Law Firm Timekeeping Survey co-sponsored by Smart WebParts and Adam Smith Esq. in 2010,[2] which the Smart WebParts team augmented by adding to it average hourly rates in order to build a business case for a timekeeping project.[3]

In this study, it is established that untimely recording of billable time results in an under-reporting of time by the timekeeper:

- Even those who record their time contemporaneously leak about 45 hours annually; and

- Those who reconstruct their time lose more than double that amount of time, at about 97 hours per year.

It seems obvious to point out, but it also *takes time* to enter time. According to the survey, the difference between the amounts of time a timekeeper takes to enter time is dramatic when we compare daily (32.4 annual hours), weekly (48 annual hours), and monthly (69.6 annual hours) entry.

On one team I worked with, we were able to build a business case for our timekeeping project based on the data from the survey, since the firm data was not easily acquired. We extrapolated, making conservative estimates as to how many of the firm's timekeepers entered time on a weekly or less frequent basis, then applying the average hourly rate of all timekeepers. We also looked at a sample that showed us when time was entered and the date the work was performed; this indicated that, with one notable exception, none of the firm's timekeepers were entering their time contemporaneously.

Using industry data allowed us to develop the business case for improving the firm's timekeeping practices at a very conservative estimated $7 million – just for doing a better job of capturing time on work they were already doing. This further facilitated the team's ability to calculate that, for every 1 percent improvement this firm made, it was worth $2 million to the firm's bottom line, without adding additional work or infrastructure. The team set a project goal of a very modest and achievable 5 percent improvement, which was exceeded. In addition to improving financial performance, a firm that begins with a timekeeping process is able to generate better data about effort that it can use in other areas, including additional process improvement projects.

This point about the usefulness of firm data and what to do about it was articulated well in an ILTA white paper by Lann Wasson of Husch Blackwell LLP: "Lean, Six Sigma and the management approaches called by their names are fundamentally rooted in measurement, so it is common practice to observe the workplace and collect data either by conducting time studies or mining existing internal databases. Unlike some other service industries, law firms are technology-rich office environments where the intellectual, social and creative work is often invisible and impossible to capture in traditional ways.

To determine whether data in the firm's time entry system could be incorporated into the value stream map, the practice group chair asked each lawyer in the pilot to identify a short list of matters from the last few years as a representative sample for comparison. Using a recent matter as a test case for analysis, the firm's financial reporting group compiled the data and graphed the results as a composition and distribution of time worked per role, per day.

After several hours of discussion with the lead partner on the deal, we concluded that there was simply no way to extrapolate the cost of process segments, much less the individual process steps, based on the existing data points. The dynamics of corporate transactions, the practice of block billing and a lack of coding had resulted in a set of unstructured data that was of little use in defining a baseline. Furthermore, given the complexity of the transactions in the sample, the opportunity cost of attempting to restructure the time entries by manually parsing the data was simply too great.

While the lack of useful hard data presented another challenge to the development of the value stream map, it also prompted a deeper discussion of the dynamics of information flow and of other more qualitative attributes of activities within each process segment. As a result of this dialogue, the team began evaluating the benefits of different forms of estimation and again reached consensus on a viable way to approximate values for cycle and lead times. Going forward, the team concluded that if lawyers started coding their time based on a defined set of project phases, data could be gleaned from the accounting system and layered onto the process map. Until then, the group would continue to focus on describing and understanding the dynamics of transactions from a Lean Six Sigma perspective in order to gain as much insight as possible."[4]

One area that very visibly demonstrates the accelerated pace of change in the industry and the need for excellent data is the increased focus on pricing: "What started as a necessity has picked up force at a quickening pace. In 2013, 67 percent of firms had a pricing officer, while another 13 percent relegated pricing responsibility to a committee. Fourteen percent did not have an officer installed and were not planning to hire for the position. Compare those figures to just one year later – 76 percent of firms tell us they currently have a person dedicated to the pricing function. Another 7 percent plan to add the position within the year, suggesting that, by 2015, 83 percent of large law firms will have a pricing officer function installed."[5]

ALM further reports that "three quarters of firms said that they currently were implementing LPM to align work with pricing models (mostly in the larger size firms), and an additional 16 percent planned to in the future. For half the firms with LPM in place, project management has fallen under the domain of the pricing department, adding to its influence within the organization. The additional responsibility makes structural sense. If a group has the charge to safeguard profitability, it needs tools to do so. Pricing works on the revenue side. Project management aids both cost control and a focus on customer perceptions of value, to avoid improving profitability at the cost of client loyalty and retention."

However, as with anything else, without good processes, both the function and the role of pricing will not be optimized. Thus, we have another example of a law firm investing in a smart idea but in silo fashion, which by design cannot yield the best results. One respondent in the ALM White Paper "who wished to remain anonymous said that his firm does 'very poorly' in collecting and analyzing data.' Some of the limitations we face [are for] various reasons,' he said. 'One is process. There is not a good process for preparation and approval and follow up of alternative fee arrangements. Another problem is documenting the fee arrangement and getting it to the right place.'"

Pricing and process improvement

Those looking for a sure sign that things are coming together can look to the Legal Marketing Association's second, very successful P3 Conference in June 2014. The P3 Conference brings together "pricing, project management and practice innovation experts to discuss the use of various tactics to explore solutions to real issues faced by law firms today".

Lindsay Griffiths, the International Lawyers Network's director of global relationship management, writing after the conference, highlights two points to "takeaway" from the event:

- Takeaway one: Pricing and process improvement can't happen in silos; and

- Takeaway two: No more "Should we do this?" but "How can we do this?"[6]

Griffiths referenced both the ALM Intelligence pricing report and the content at P3 in her post, writing that she had read through the ALM Report "in preparation for the conference, and the main thing that struck me is that we're only now seeing an increase in integrating process management with pricing. Tim Corcoran (who was on a unique panel at P3 with Catherine MacDonagh, John Byrne and Amy Hrehovcik) put it perfectly in a post-conference interview he conducted with LexBlog: 'We spend all this time coming up with the right budget, and then we go deliver the work the same old way and we don't adhere to the budget. And either the client says "I don't want to pay anymore" or we end up taking a hit to our profits because we can't bill more but we spent more time working than we needed to.'"

Griffiths goes on to ask, "In order to meet the demands of clients to give them work more cost-effectively while maximizing the firm's profitability, it's essential to consider both of these pieces together. About 75 percent of large firms have or are working to integrate these, but is that the case at your firm? As we know, moving the needle forward within law firms takes time – it's like turning an ocean liner around. But it's worth the effort, because we're talking about making smart changes that will benefit clients AND make law firms more profitable, and who doesn't like a win-win?"

By now, I hope this report has clearly established that Lean Sigma helps us to determine the best way to carry out a certain kind of work to achieve efficiency, excellent quality of work and service, high probability of successful outcomes, and predictability. As I've suggested, though it is simple, process improvement is not easy. In fact, process improvement is hard work – to succeed, initial projects must be recognized priorities within the firm. Prioritization means that a project is resourced for rapid progress, supported by experienced Lean Six Sigma practitioners, and provided management attention on a regular basis. One way to make the case for process improvement to decision-makers is to gather data to show that the current process has plenty of waste and opportunity, discuss the benefits to the clients and firm of improving the process, and find an interested and supportive sponsor.[7]

Fixed fees demand greater efficiency

Using data as evidence, you might start with looking at pricing and the fee arrangements in your firm. According to Six Sigma Black Belt Micah Ascano, managing partner at Artifex Legal: "A simple way to think of how a process or legal service can be done with fewer billable hours is a flat fee or collared fee arrangement. Why? Because if we have a flat fee arrangement with a client, and are more efficient with our work (not more sloppy or reduced quality), the amount of savings internally (money/time) turns into extra profit or additional capacity for more clients without reducing the current level of profits for partners. To start, a law firm should focus on accurate prediction of legal costs in order to establish a baseline for measurable process improvements. Then, once the return on investment of the process improvement has occurred, the firm can make a strategic decision on whether or not to share that measurable cost savings with the client."[8]

For law firms trying to deliver better value to clients, Lisa Damon of Seyfarth Shaw offers the following suggestions:

- Be willing to invest and commit to changing for the long haul;

- Ensure you have commitment from the top;

- Find client advocates who will help champion your cause; and

- Accept small successes at first. Change comes slowly for many lawyers, and organizational change does not happen rapidly.[9]

One of the most important things we can do is to use our client's definitions of value and quality; firms must look at their business from the client's perspective, not their own. By understanding the case, matter, or transaction lifecycle from the client's needs and processes, we can discover what they are seeing and feeling. When we have this knowledge, we can identify areas where we can add significant value or improvement from their perspective.

"I think most clients would be okay with the idea that firms [that] would learn how to be more efficient would take a little more in profit, as long as that profit isn't an increase in costs to the client, in exchange for the security of a flat fee for the business savvy client. Long term, once cost savings is calculable to the firm, that savings can then be passed on to the client. Again, what business client will balk [at the idea] that if the firm takes the risk with a flat fee, it should be rewarded with additional profit, barring a complete windfall, if it tries to learn how to be more efficient?"[10]

Firms are getting ever more creative about how they are responding to clients' needs. One recent example is Torys LLP, which is opening a small "insourcing" office called Torys Legal Services Centre with expected opening in the fall of 2014. This is where the firm will perform high-volume, recurring legal work such as reviewing contracts or performing due diligence on corporate deals for the firm's established corporate clients.

The Torys Legal Services Centre "will be charged with developing new, more efficient ways of doing this kind of legal work that can then be rolled out across the rest of the firm, which has offices in Toronto, New York, Calgary and Montreal... The move comes as debate over new ways of doing business continue to ripple through the legal profession. The corporate clients that use the country's elite law firms are increasingly demanding they curb the spiraling costs that come with $800-an-hour senior partners, or provide more predictable legal bills with fixed fees or flat rates.

Torys says its plan is unique in Canada, although British firm Allen & Overy opened a similar office in Belfast in 2011, where it also moved human resources and other support staff to cut costs… Mr. Fowles, who articled at Torys in 1994, said the new office is simply a response to client demands: 'They want to know upfront what things are going to cost and we'll be able to tell them, and they will be able to rely on it.'"[11]

At the Legal Lean Sigma Institute, when we get started with skill development we also begin using the client's perspective and a data-based approach to identify potential projects to use in tailoring our certification courses. The firm identifies a portfolio of potential/high-impact projects and then carefully selects cross-functional teams and team leaders who would carry out each project if the firm decides to improve that process following the course. Our goal is for the participants to successfully complete the course and then to participate in the first project(s). We accomplish this by providing the teams with an opportunity to begin applying the concepts they are learning in our courses. They draft elements of their process improvement projects, such as project charters and rough process maps in the class together. They also earn a White or Yellow Belt in Legal Lean Sigma, or a combined Legal Lean Sigma and project management certification. Additionally, we work with firms to apply for continuing legal education credits and have always been approved. As such, we accomplish many things simultaneously with this approach.

Moreover, because most of the exercises in these tailored courses will deal with the particular projects the firm is considering, firms have additional information, such as draft business cases, problem/opportunity statements, and process maps, to use in making the determination as to which projects will be selected. Subsequently, the teams carry out their projects, aided by an experienced Lean Sigma facilitator/practitioner, as they work their way through the DMAIC (define, measure, analyze, improve, control) methodology. We believe that it is best for the firm's internal resources to carry out as many of the team leadership and facilitation tasks as they possibly can. The role of the facilitator is to support the project and team, coach the team leader, and provide feedback to the team, champion, and steering committee along the way. The facilitator's aim is to ensure the successful delivery of the project, accelerated skill development, and strategic implementation that enhances the ability to create competitive advantages and lasting transformations for the firm through cultural change.

The LPM initiative at Thompson Hine

Thompson Hine's long-term investment in culture change began some years ago with its then-industry-leading "client service pledge". The pledge foreshadowed many of the concerns about lawyers that clients have articulated since the great recession. Recognizing the pledge was only part of the solution, managing partner Deborah Read convened a committee of senior partners and firm leaders to steer the firm's program, focusing on further elevating service delivery. Important areas of focus included legal project management (LPM), alternative staffing models, value-based billing, and efficiency.

The LPM initiative at Thompson Hine began with an assessment of the existing tools, client interest, and available internal resources. The first major undertaking was the creation of a proprietary task code set by practice group, followed by mandatory task coding for all time entries. Task coding was surrounded by a series of metrics with each practice group receiving a twice-yearly review of its performance against those metrics. The steering group retained a consultant to help the firm establish the business case and educate the partnership on general principles of LPM. A consultant was then used to educate a select group of partners on LPM and to coach them through a series of pilot projects. After assessing the results of the training and the pilot projects, the steering group concluded that a dedicated internal resource was necessary to drive adoption and sustainable change at the pace the business case demanded.

A C-suite-level director of LPM was hired, and a dedicated pricing manager was put in place. The director of LPM reviewed the steering group's prior work and developed a project plan for adoption and culture change. Among his first undertakings was driving conclusion to a pending decision regarding financial/project management systems. In parallel to the implementation of the financial/project management systems, the firm undertook development of:

1. A proprietary "friendly front end" budgeting application;

2. A proprietary educational resource and LPM template repository;

3. A standard set of periodic LPM reports available for any engagement; and

4. A standard packet of materials used to educate clients and firm personnel on the firm's capabilities.

The firm also sought frequent client feedback on the direction of the initiative, which resulted in some fine-tuning of the structure and the message.

Simultaneously, the firm deployed LPM techniques in pending engagements, selected with an eye toward team leaders who would be early adopters and internal evangelists. The LPM team draws from resources across a matrixed organization, including information systems, finance, and marketing and strategy, to support legal teams. Where the engagement justifies it, a dedicated project management resource is added to the legal team. Metrics surround those teams and there are quarterly assessments by the firm's executive committee on progress and resources.

The firm's deployment of LPM, and the metrics surrounding it, are closely tied to the way value-based fee arrangements are developed and managed, how staffing is adapting to current market imperatives, and how processes are examined and continuously refined. Thompson Hine continues to make progress across all four fronts, integrating each of these components into a unified service delivery model.

Three approaches to process improvement in law firms

The Legal Lean Sigma Institute conducted a study in May 2012 and I co-authored the published results with Laura Colcord in a white paper entitled "Three Approaches to Process Improvement". Many questions we asked were about the different approaches law firms were taking with regard to employing process improvement for competitive advantage. Each firm really is unique and there is no one right way to do this work. However, over the last several years, we have seen law firms initially approach process improvement in the following three, primary ways:

1. Strategic/organizational development;

2. Education and skill development; and

3. Demonstration projects.

It is currently only a small number of law firms that have made a strategic decision or done organizational structuring at a firm, department, or practice group level. Some, however, have made a strategic decision to begin bringing process improvement into their firm because of a strong belief that there will be competitive advantages to building deep process improvement disciplines and skills into the organization.

The objectives of such a program are to:

1. Comprehensively redesign the processes of a business, to make them as capable and efficient as possible and transform the performance of the business; and

2. Build the capacity and infrastructure for ongoing change. Some of the elements to support a systematic change program may be naturally present in the firm. To create the others, the program must include activities to build them.

The eight key elements to support a strategic approach to process improvement are:

1. Process perspective – Performance targets and measurements for processes;

2. Clear need and goals for change – Documented and communicated as a "compelling case", cascaded goals;

3. Assessment process established to create a change plan – Value stream mapping or baselining, resulting in a documented change plan;

4. Change skills and tools – Leadership training, change agent training, and awareness training for the general employee population, mentoring to supplement skills;

5. Improvement culture – Identification of role models, support for change agents/teams;

6. Knowledge-building – Symposia to share learning, knowledge management system;

7. Benefits capture – Measurement systems to monitor and track benefits delivery; and

8. Change infrastructure – Site steering committees, extensive communication, goals linked to employee objectives.

Thus, a strategic approach involves strategy and goal setting, discussions and decisions about roles and responsibilities related to both process improvement and project management, developing an approach to skills development that includes training, mentorship, and project experience, determining a project selection and prioritization method that works for the particular firm, and establishing a process improvement steering committee.

Typically, then, members of the firm's management committee will receive some level of training as part of this approach and several key constituencies will need specific skills in order to support and drive change:

- Leaders must be capable of communicating the need for change and the vision of the future, steering change teams, eliminating roadblocks, and modeling new behaviors;

- Facilitators/change agents within the firm will need skills in specific Lean Six Sigma tools, change agency, team leadership, and project management;

- Team leader training is delivered to firms that are interested in developing people to lead projects and focuses on facilitation, project management, change agency, and project communication skills; and

- Staff in general will need some facility with Lean Sigma tools, as well as detailed process knowledge and interest in improving their processes.

Many firms begin with education and skill development. They start by selecting lawyers and business professionals to participate in programs such as our White or Yellow Belt certification courses. The objective is to begin generating interest in and developing knowledge about Lean and Six Sigma as they specifically relate to the legal profession.

Legal Lean Sigma training methods and qualifications

Ideally, at the Legal Lean Sigma Institute, we prefer to combine classroom training with real-world experience on projects that will benefit the firm (and its clients – there is an excellent example of how Morgan Lewis has approached combined training with their clients in Chapter 9). Our preferred approach to beginning this skills development is to select a portfolio of high-impact projects, with careful selection of teams and team leaders who will carry out the projects and then to begin to develop the skills that will allow them to carry out subsequent projects.

Amy Hrehovcik of Ailey Advisors suggests: "While fear of failure is universal, the less accustomed a person is to failing, the larger this fear becomes. By creating a safe environment where the law firm engages each other and their clients in process conversations, they begin to develop muscles that have been dormant and realize that employees and clients are craving these dialogues. The structure of the Legal Lean Sigma courses and project gives a voice and a platform to all members of the team in a way that levels the playing field. Emotion is removed from communication, frustration is reduced and firms demonstrate respect for their workers and clients by not pretending to understand their wishes better than they do."

Typically, this foundational knowledge allows firms to identify opportunities for process improvement and to begin to apply process improvement concepts, all while keeping the client perspective at the forefront. It is significantly easier to do this when a common language and understanding is established.

Seyfarth's reports indicate, for example, that every lawyer and staff member has now been trained in basic Lean, and the firm is rolling out Yellow Belt training for various departments on specific competencies. Senior leaders have all received advanced training as well. At the Legal Lean Sigma Institute, any certified Yellow Belt team members who successfully complete a project may be awarded a Green Belt certification in Legal Lean Sigma.

Finally, another approach that law firms are taking is simply to try a project to see what Lean Sigma is all about and how it might work best in their organization. Initially some of our clients are unsure as to whether process improvement is advantageous enough to provide a good return on investment, unwilling to make the significant training investment at the outset, or simply just want to begin right away. These clients often prefer to start with minimal training followed by a demonstration project to assess the methodologies, the results, and the fit of Lean Sigma with the firm's culture.

If a firm elects to proceed in this manner, without the support of the classroom training to provide context and frameworks and begin developing skills internally, we are always obligated to suggest that the projects will rely in largest measure on expert facilitation from experienced external consultants to lead the projects and deliver the results. In this case, our expectations should be limited to providing a robust demonstration of the power of the Lean Sigma methodology, with results that provide a good return on the investment.

Conventionally, a project is selected and the standard DMAIC process is carried out, after which the firm evaluates both the success of the project and the ability of process improvement to deliver benefits to the firm. After successful project completion, the firm may choose to discuss a more in-depth approach that will not only provide project results, but will also transfer skills and knowledge so that the firm starts down the path toward self-sufficiency in process improvement and project management skills.

The treatment that we have found particularly useful in the law firm environment is the Kaizen methodology (see Chapter 3). This approach allows a tightly scoped project to be delivered in a compressed time period. Because law firms usually prefer to start and finish things quickly once they have made a decision to move forward, we have found that the Kaizen approach is very appealing to our clients.

Regardless, to get started and structure for success, it is important to consider firm culture, drivers, and any misconceptions that exist, including the ideas that "In order to win professionally, someone else must lose, that creativity and innovation are bi-products of speed and uninhibited and unstructured, workflows," as Amy Hrehovcik says. "Others include the beliefs that there is no process, that talented people can overcome a broken process, and that what we're doing is working."

In the words of Jim Collins: "The great task, rarely achieved, is to blend creative intensity with relentless discipline so as to amplify the creativity rather than destroy it. When you marry operating excellence with innovation, you multiply the value of your creativity."

Because each law firm (and each client) is unique, there is no one right way to employ PI and PM in a law firm. While some firms and service providers have made their work visible, others are engaged in efforts well under the radar. Nonetheless, that evidence exists to suggest that all three approaches produce successes and certainly position firms that employ PI and PM to great competitive advantage.

Conclusion

Regardless of the approach used, the tools of process improvement and project management work very well in a law firm environment. The DMAIC structure is effective for many reasons: it is logical and rigorous, requiring us to exercise great discipline and encouraging us to be our most creative within a rigorous framework. This translates to operating excellence and innovation.

Whatever you decide to do, do not delay. The rate of change is not slowing down. And for every firm included in this report, there are others who are quietly employing Lean Six Sigma for competitive advantage; it would not be unreasonable to think that we may hear about them in the very near future, and that the use of these key process improvement methodologies is moving closer to mainstream every day. In any case,

Lean Six Sigma offers a great opportunity to be an architect and design the way you do legal work in a way that delivers value to all concerned.

References

1. Corcoran, T. B., "The 2 Critical Questions that Lead to Continuous Improvement", 17 December 2012; see www.corcoranlawbizblog.com/2012/12/the-2-critical-questions.

2. Gerstein, T., "Recommendation for Law Firm Timekeeping Best Practices", Smart WebParts LLC, 2010; see www.smart-webparts.com/pdfs/timekeepingbest-practices.pdf.

3. Gerstein, T., "The Agony of Unbooked Time" (blog post), *Smart Time Time Keeping Blog*, 31 August 2010; see http://blog.smart-webparts.com/page/13.

4. Wasson, L., "An Unconventional Alliance: Lessons from a Lean Six Sigma Pilot", ITLA, June 2011.

5. ALM Legal Intelligence's 2014 Special Report, "Pricing Professionals: Essential to Law Firms, An Ally to Clients", June 2014.

6. Griffiths, L., "Two for Tuesdays: Takeaways from the LMA's P3 Conference", *Zen and the Art of Legal Marketing*, 17 June 2014; see www.zenlegalnetworking.com/2014/06/articles/two-for-tuesdays/two-for-tuesdays-takeaways-from-p3.

7. In his book *The Legal Process Improvement Toolkit* (Ark Group, 2012), Mark Bull provides a 12 tool starter kit outlining the primary methodologies for delivering process improvement within your firm. These include how to build a simple process map of your organization; identify critical legal business processes; use models to assess process maturity; use Six Sigma to improve the quality of your process outputs; analyze the potential causes and effects of process problems; deliver process efficiencies using lean principles; capture and use VOC (voice of the client) data; and implement LPI as a fundamental component of a successful legal project management program.

8. Ascano, M., "Statistics and the Flat Fee Part 1: The Theory", *Small Firm Innovation*; see www.smallfirminnovation.com/2013/04/statistics-and-the-flat-fee-part-1-the-theory.

9. Duncan, S. S., "5 Firms Take Bold Approaches", *ABA Law Practice* magazine, volume 38, No. 6, November/December 2012; see www.americanbar.org/publications/law_practice_magazine/2012/november-december/5-firms-take-bold-approaches.html.

10. See n. 8, above.

11. Gray, J., "Bay Street law firm launches legal 'incubator' in Halifax", *The Globe and Mail*, 1 July, 2014.

Chapter 8:
Creating a Lean Sigma culture of continuous improvement

We already know that most of our processes are falling far short of their potential and that improving them will benefit all concerned. We also know that changes in the business environment are constant. In fact, they are taking place at an ever-increasing rate. Clients keep saying they want their law firms to speak their language, be their business partner, anticipate their needs, and provide greater predictability. There are some excellent examples of firms that are providing excellent responses to those needs.

Accordingly, all of the fast-paced changes in the business environment and increasing client demands create ever-greater requirements for even higher process capabilities and process efficiencies. Once we make things better, requirements and changes will drive us to improve again. This explains why continuous improvement is an endless cycle and must eventually become part of a firm's culture in order to develop and sustain competitive edge. By embracing Lean Sigma, firms create a culture of continuous improvement; this enables them to avoid performance gaps and even to create opportunities for innovation and competitive edge.

Writing in *The Financial Post*, Denise Deveau suggests that achieving an internal culture change is something that requires patience and a consistent commitment from the top down. Laura Croucher, partner with KPMG Management Consulting, tells Denise that "management tools and processes... play a key role in driving cultural change, including performance management and measurement, training, and hiring for fit."[1]

"Changing a culture is especially difficult in the legal space. Talent is razor sharp and seems to dissect improvement efforts for sport. Plus, governing bodies view 'non-lawyer' expertise as subpar, and partners continue to be slow to adapt. The 2014 Law Firms in Transition survey reports that only 7 percent of firm leaders think their partners are highly aware that the industry is even changing. For those who are at all competitive, this is a statistic that should create serious drive", says Amy

Hrehovcik, founder of Ailey Advisors and consultant affiliated with the Legal Lean Sigma Institute.

She reminds us that "a practical approach trumps a theoretical one; this is why the Yellow Belt certification courses are the way to go. They are even better when they include clients." All of our clients tell us that, just like most things, building momentum requires maximum effort at the beginning. By involving clients, there appears to be lighter lifting in terms of driving cultural change. As one client reported, "Legal Lean Sigma's collaborative Yellow Belt is the perfect opportunity to differentiate the firm in the eyes of the client, and serves as the primary catalyst to change the firm culture as it creates an environment where people change themselves."

Employing Lean Six Sigma for continuous improvement

One of the principles of Lean Sigma is to align and empower employees. This is a key idea for developing and sustaining a culture of continuous improvement and, obviously, there are many ways to accomplish this – not every law firm is quite ready to become the type of environment where we all stop using the offensive term "non-lawyer".

Valorem Law Group "operates in a family-like setting. Ideas and new approaches are welcomed and expected through biweekly 'collab-o-storms' with all lawyers and staff", says founder Pat Lamb. In fact, the firm shows use of a registered trademark in Collab-O-Storm, suggesting that their approach, and name for it, really is unique.

Structured more traditionally, Ogletree Deakins took a different approach and created a Lean Sigma culture starting in 2010, when it began the process of immersing managers and employees in Lean Sigma principles and practices by working with consultants who were experts in Lean Sigma and in legal and professional services organizations.

According to Sharon M. Wardrip, chief administrative officer, "While working on actual firm processes, we were able to obtain Yellow Belt, Green Belt and Team Leader certifications. By using proven, disciplined approaches, tools, and skills, we have increased productivity and efficiency, positively affected our bottom line, and identified and reduced costs and errors in our existing processes."

Ogletree has utilized the define, measure, analyze, improve, and control approach in applications that include timekeeping, billing, RFP responses, record retention, lateral partner onboarding, and litigation management. Wardrip explains: "More than a program or a catch phrase, Lean Sigma became a way of thinking differently about work processes and discovering more creative improvements and solutions. Every day our firm is faced with new challenges and opportunities to maximize efficiencies. We will continue to develop and employ strategies and tactics based on the client perspective. Lean Sigma methods have given us the tools for each of us to take our role, our departments and our firm to a new level of excellence."

In their article on culture change through Lean Sigma, the Measure by Measure Consulting firm asked: "[A]s Lean Six Sigma practitioners, why should we care about culture?"[2] They answered that, based on their experience: "[W]e believe that top management understands the importance of values and cultures but prioritizes cultural change efforts low because of the perceived resistance, disparate consulting approaches, length of the effort and correspondingly low probability of success... Lean Six Sigma consultants are uniquely positioned to approach cultural change from a fresh perspective. Our experience... and follow-up research taught us that culture change is path dependent and that high trust/high cooperation cultures desired by so many senior management teams require the foundational discipline and support that is embodied in the Lean Six Sigma principles. The new Lean Six Sigma professionals can assist senior management in designing and implementing the systems, measurements, processes, and controls that will provide the foundational support for the high trust / high cooperation cultures required in the 21st century."

Driving process improvement

Ideally, an organization will have a methodology for agreeing on the processes that could most benefit from process improvement work. Conceptually, a comprehensive process scorecard which compares processes across all key dimensions might be used to identify opportunities. Organizations seldom have this organized a view of their processes and so a less comprehensive, but still systematic methodology called a "baseline assessment" is often used. However, in the early stages of a process improvement program, projects are most commonly selected based on purely practical considerations.

Progress along the continuum does not happen automatically; leaders must deliberately choose to build organizational capability and accrue permanent benefits. At Thompson Hine, the drive for continuous improvement is part carrot and part stick. Moving the culture at the firm has required:

1. Senior firm management involvement;

2. Development and reporting of metrics;

3. Continuous multi modal messaging;

4. Client support for initiatives; and

5. Mandatory participation in some program elements.

Deborah Read, the firm's managing partner, and the firm's executive committee lead by example in driving for continuous improvement. Each senior lawyer and practice group chair is "all in", committing to continuous improvement and legal project management of their own engagements and to developing appropriate processes in their own departments. The firm tracks a number of metrics to show adoption and effectiveness of its LPM initiatives. Partners receive reports on these qualitative and quantitative metrics at least quarterly and sometimes monthly when developments demand. The metrics are designed to ensure that not only are legal engagements measured for improvements but also that the process improvement and project management initiatives are themselves measured for continuous improvement.

Multimodal messaging about adoption of firm initiatives, successes, tools, and training is also a key strategy for creating the culture of continuous improvement. Read: the firm's executive committee and practice group leaders, senior staff across all departments, and internal communications tools all drive home the message of the business case for culture change and the tools available to shorten the trip. The communications all highlight early adopters and their success stories at firm-wide events or in firm-wide communications. Clients have also been recruited as internal evangelists and have even participated in internal workshops on skills development.

Finally, some of the elements driving culture change are simply not optional. The firm's proprietary task code sets are mandatory for time entry. Senior level approval of certain fee arrangements is mandatory, and adoption of LPM techniques which drive continuous improvement is often a condition of approval. The firm's proprietary financial reporting protocols generate budget-to-actual reporting on a monthly basis – whether or not the lead partner or client have requested it. This reporting can be an early warning system for projects in need of extra attention. Experience has shown the value of linking systems and tools like the matter intake system, docketing tools, and budgeting tools to the financial and matter management systems so that partners and administrators get a unified picture of where cases are at and where they are headed.

Organizations have many processes, nearly all of which could benefit from improvements. Again, process improvement is not easy – for any hope of success, key leaders must agree on which processes have priority for improvement and will ensure that projects receive the right resources and management support and attention on a regular basis.

The ROI of process improvement

Making process changes does not necessarily translate into improvements in the desired metrics or the bottom line. Often, managers need to get involved to translate a process improvement into a financial benefit – and a process improvement may generate more than one kind of benefit. Determining return on investment requires us to consider the tangible returns, such as increased client satisfaction with process and outcomes leading to repeat business and referrals, more efficient process (we can handle more business with the same number of employees), and fewer out-of-pocket costs for a process. There are also intangible returns, such as increased client satisfaction and goodwill, increased employee satisfaction and morale, and increased reputation for professionalism and results.

The benefits achieved by process improvement can – and should – be sustained. It takes time, resources, and commitment to the process of process improvement to create a culture of continuous improvement. We know that "culture beats strategy" – but we can create a strategy to develop a culture of continuous improvement.

By developing a firm-wide approach to employing the methodologies and tools of Lean Six Sigma, we can more easily reach consensus and clarity around the selection and prioritization of our projects and project teams. By first evaluating our processes and prioritizing by determining which processes (and then which aspects of them) most need attention, we are able to begin to develop our plans, messaging, approaches, leaders, champions, stakeholders, skills, and teams that span the firm.

Plus, by working together as high-functioning, cross-departmental, diverse teams, we improve by employing the DMAIC framework and Lean and Six Sigma tools to bring the process to the required performance and efficiency levels. Many teams report that working on a project in this fashion is one of the best work experiences they have had. Those who become educated and experienced in Lean Six Sigma never see the firm (or the world) in the same way again. For one thing, they see that *everything* can be improved. They are encouraged and empowered to not just think, but to ask "why" and "what if" more often. They are not as quick to accept "that's the way we have always done it" as the reason for continuing to perform in a particular way. They are also less likely to treat comments that begin with "anecdotally..." as evidence for what is or is not working in a process.

Lean Six Sigma thinking is grounded first in learning what a client finds valuable about a process, so it is inherently supportive of a "client-focused" or "client-centered" culture, which nearly every firm boasts in its marketing materials. At this point, clients are less impressed with talk: they want specificity with regard to the behaviors in which the firm engages that demonstrate a commitment to that promise.

After improving processes at the firm, we do not rest on our laurels; we repeat so that we can claim that our firm is the very best it can be. Because the best law firms, the best lawyers, and the best business professionals are always interested in getting better.

References

1. Deveau, D., "How to convince workers you actually care about what they think", *Financial Post*, 28 May 2014; see http://business.financialpost.com/2014/05/28/how-to-convince-workers-you-actually-care-about-what-they-think/?__federated=1.
2. Measure by Measure Consulting LLC, "Why Culture Change May Be Lean Six Sigma's Greatest Value: One Award Winning Company Discovered the True Value of Lean Six Sigma", 15 February 2010.

Chapter 9:
Lean Six Sigma and the client connection – Changing the conversation

When clients say they want lawyers who can speak their language, be their business advisor, and understand their goals, Lean Six Sigma principles and methodologies can help change the conversation. Amy Hrehovcik says: "Serious lip service is given to defining value in the eyes of the client, but it is rare to find a system that gathers this feedback that is not based on the Lean Sigma principles and framework."

John Grant has a value theory that is represented by the equation:

$$Value = Benefit - Investment$$

Writing on his *Legal Value Theory* blog, he says that "the challenge is twofold: (1) How to figure out what will truly benefit the Customer and (2) How to get the Customer to increase its investment in order to obtain that Benefit. This is where Susskind's Disruption stage comes into play. Disruptive Providers will be those who figure out how to create new ways of increasing Value by delivering greater customer Benefit and capturing additional Customer Investment (fees) from the gains. And this is also where I think the true value of Lean can shine."[1]

He goes on to share his perspective on Lean by suggesting that "its core purpose is not its drive for efficiency, but its focus on understanding Customer needs. Lean tools like Voice of the Customer Analysis and SIPOC charts, along with Agile tools like User Stories, can help Providers understand their Customer's Value premise and craft solutions around those discoveries. The key is to truly understand what the Customer needs, not just what it is looking for. That is no easy task; what the Customer says it wants and what it really needs are not always aligned. Digging deep to understand the Customer's fundamentals is critical, and you're not done there. Next you need to consider the best possible way to deliver Benefit based on those needs, and it may not be the way you, or the customer, have always done things.

But if disruption were easy, everyone would be doing it. So my overall point is that efficiency is good, but figuring out how to change the game is much better. Fortunately, lawyers who learn how to use tool sets from Lean, Agile, and elsewhere can do both."[2]

The value focus

Process improvement methodologies like Lean and Six Sigma have spread to virtually every industry in the world. A 2007 research study from trade publication *iSixSigma* magazine estimated that over half of Fortune 500 and as many as 82 percent of Fortune 100 companies have used Six Sigma methodologies to produce savings that total roughly $427 billion.[3] With numbers like these, it is no wonder that we are seeing requests for proposals, which, in addition to requiring responding law firms to discuss their own process improvement and project management frameworks (some ask about process management), also ask candidate firms questions such as: "What changes could we implement in our company to make the work for us more cost-efficient?"

ALM Legal Intelligence found that "the concept of value is entering conversations with clients at least some of the time for 86 percent of firms. It is the beginning of an educational effort that might eventually move the industry from an hourly focus to one of value, although a change is far from certain. Legal work has such a long history of hourly billing, getting beyond the concept means changing the minds of many – never an easy task. Most seriously, the basic drives to focus on value and gain insight into profitability still have a significant road ahead. More than half of firms tell us that at least some of the time the end game of pricing work with clients usually turns into 'getting a good price' rather than understanding the cost structure of a matter."[4]

With challenges this clear, and questions this pointed, what law firm would not want to embrace Lean Six Sigma and use it to make their own businesses better; deliver better value to customers; and employ the framework provided by process improvement to connect with clients in novel and more deeply satisfying ways?

For example, Foley & Lardner may have a long history of working with manufacturing clients, but it was only recently that a Foley lawyer participated in a Kaizen with a firm client. This work took place at the client site – and the process addressed was in manufacturing, not legal. The insights gained and relationships built through this experience were significant.

Legal departments, law firms, and service providers have not been sitting around, waiting to take action and work more closely with clients on service issues. However, a much more intense focus was brought to bear on the "value" conversation in 2008, when the Association of Corporate Counsel (ACC) introduced its Value Challenge, "an initiative to reconnect the value and the cost of legal services".

The ACC stated that: "[T]here are many ways to improve value in the firm-client relationship. The ACC Value Challenge focuses on providing resources and training – for law firms as well as law departments – on these key value levers: Aligning Relationships, Value-based Fee Structures – i.e. not based on the "billable hour," Staffing and Training Practices, Budgeting, Project Management, Process Improvement, Use of Technology, Data Management, Knowledge Management and Change Management." It is worth pointing out that firms that embrace process improvement and project management and perform well are also more likely to perform better in all the other dimensions.

Providing legal services in a fundamentally different way

Susan Duncan returned to her consulting practice at the RainMaking Oasis (of which she is a founder) after serving as the chief strategy and development officer of Squire Sanders – a 1,300-lawyer, Global 15 law firm with 36 offices in 17 countries. Among the highlights of her work at Squire Sanders was her involvement with the integration of two mergers in 12 months; a refocus of the firm's client service and value initiative, including the introduction of client interviews and a new Covenant with Clients; and the roll out of a new planning process that resulted in 56 practice group, industry group, and regional business plans that also correlated budgeting with measurable objectives.

Seyfarth Shaw

In an article for the ABA's *Law Practice* magazine,[5] Duncan interviewed Lisa Damon, a partner and catalyst for the Seyfarth*Lean* initiative. Damon shared insight about the firm's goal to "drive better business outcomes for clients by providing legal services in a fundamentally different way". She explained that "process improvement begins with listening. Seyfarth's approach incorporates 'voice of the client' techniques throughout the process to help establish clear goals, desired business outcomes, and benchmarks for measuring success". Seyfarth works with clients on their extensive use of process mapping, which encompasses data collection, engagement planning, work assignment, and resource management to help ensure that the legal strategy and desired outcomes support the client's objectives.

In 2011 Seyfarth Shaw established a consultancy that advises in-house departments on how to apply Lean and manage outside work. In other words, they have a separate business where they are teaching their clients about process improvement and helping them to become more efficient. Additionally, the lawyers in the firm are able to use process mapping and other Six Sigma approaches to identify and understand the underlying costs of providing different kinds of work. They say "this allows productive two-way conversations between the firm and clients on how to achieve the best results, align costs to value, and provides a transparent pricing package… This enables clients to understand quickly what steps are involved in meeting their objectives."

Eversheds

Graham Richardson and Martin Hopkins of Eversheds, which has 1,200 lawyers, were also interviewed by Duncan for the article, reporting that the firm "has been pioneering new and better approaches to delivering legal services for the past decade…". Duncan found that, from project management and process improvement to pricing and budget predictability, the firm continually innovates to improve its services and value to clients, using project management as "the framework for its six-year-old groundbreaking relationship with Tyco, and most recently a similar arrangement with Eni. Eversheds has applied a data-rich metric approach to delivering and managing services for these two companies in multiple global jurisdictions on a fixed-fee basis. For all clients, lawyers apply process-mapping approaches that align the clients' objectives with strategy and cost."

The Pfizer Legal Alliance

Duncan also wrote about The Pfizer Legal Alliance: "Nineteen law firms, working together to advance the value of legal counseling to benefit all Alliance partners, their clients and the legal profession". In a 2012 article, she reported, "Since its inception three years ago, the Pfizer Legal Alliance, an innovative partnering strategy, continues to be highly effective both for Pfizer and for the 19 law firms currently selected as members."[6]

The article featured highlights from a roundtable hosted by Bucerius Law School's Center on the Legal Profession at the offices of Venable in New York City at which Ellen Rosenthal, chief counsel of Pfizer Legal

Alliance (PLA); Jeff Chasnow, chief counsel emerging markets; and John Dougherty, partner at DLA Piper, shared their observations of the program's challenges and successes.

These highlights covered:

- Key features/components of the Pfizer Legal Alliance: Fee structures, performance reviews, team composition, training and development, and a knowledge-sharing platform;
- The benefits to Pfizer: Predictability of their annual legal budget and substantially reduced annual legal spending; and
- Benefits to alliance law firms: A steady flow of work, more total work/revenue, and, if efficient, matters are resolved quickly and are more profitable. Firms also use their participation "as a driver of change in pricing and measurement of value away from hours, onto efficiency and results".

Duncan also interviewed a number of thought-leaders for an article focused on firms looking to adapt and innovate.[7] One thought leader, Mike Roster, former chair of the ACC, former GC, and former AmLaw 20 partner, said that: "Whether functioning as inside or outside counsel, you've got to aim for at least one of these three targets: reduce legal cost (in-house and outside combined) by 25 percent, provide near certainty in cost, and/or significantly and measurably improve outcomes. If you're not achieving at least one of these targets, just what is it you are trying to accomplish?"

Duncan concludes with some solid advice from the late Dr John Martin, chairman of Chadwick Martin and Bailey, and partner at South Street Strategy Group. He said, that "to avoid obstacles to innovation, law firms should follow these steps:

- Establish a common definition/understanding of what innovation means for their firms as well as for their clients.
- Develop a systematic approach and framework for innovation.
- Look forward, not backward. Stop looking at the past for proof and precedents and look to the future for new ideas and solutions. Similarly, stop following and start leading.
- Identify and deal with the barriers."

A collaborative approach to process improvement

Interestingly, every two years, Process Excellence Network (PEX Network) undertakes a "State of the Industry" research project to better understand general trends in how companies are approaching operational excellence. In 2013, PEX Network conducted this survey to better understand emerging trends in process excellence, asking: "What tools and methodologies are companies using in their approach to process excellence? What is the outlook for budgets and resources? What are the general trends practitioners are experiencing? What are the skills and capabilities that are in demand?"

PEX reported that only "12.1% of the 800+ process professionals who responded to the survey report that the legal department was one of the areas where they were applying continuous improvement. Raytheon, Tyco International, John Deere, and DuPont are a few of the companies that are widely acknowledged to have used Lean Six Sigma within their legal departments."[8] For instance, DuPont's legal process model applies Six Sigma to increase efficiency, reduce costs, and manage risks. They have successfully applied the techniques to improving processes to various areas, such as litigation and patents, and have run Green Belt projects every year.

It bears restating then: there are significant opportunities for law firms to not only use Lean Six Sigma in their own businesses, but also to work with the many legal departments that have not yet learned about or employed process improvement methodologies. These clients (or prospective clients) would be better served by lawyers, law firms, and other service providers who introduce them to these transformational approaches and then employ these in a collaborative fashion. As has been suggested repeatedly in this book, the firms that do so proactively are not only going to get a better process, they are more likely to have a much better client relationship at the end of the day.

The eData group at Morgan Lewis

One stellar example of such an approach was employed by the e-Data group at Morgan Lewis. "I first became interested in using Lean and Six Sigma in my practice group after earning my Legal Lean Sigma Yellow Belt certification while obtaining a Master's in Law Firm Management at The George Washington University", said Stephanie A. "Tess" Blair, partner in and leader of Morgan Lewis's eData Practice.

"In short order, I determined my goal: to have everyone in my group trained and certified in Legal Lean Sigma. First, I arranged for private delivery of the same Yellow Belt certification course to a core group in the eData practice. Then, some of those Yellow Belts were trained to serve as facilitators to support instructors at one day White Belt programs in seven offices. This approach allowed us to train nearly everyone in our practice – over 100 in number – in seven offices very quickly. This not only provided everyone with a common vocabulary, but supported a critical shift in thinking about how we work with clients and do our work both with them and each other."

Following the skill development of the entire practice group, two cross-functional project teams were carefully selected and formed. Each team went through Kaizen training and worked on their two selected projects in December 2011, which were tightly scoped so as to be suitable for the Kaizen approach. The two teams moved through the DMAIC phases in an accelerated workshop fashion.

The project work was set up so that the teams worked at the same time, with two different expert consultants, in separate rooms at the same office. The teams met at the end of each day to observe each other's gate reviews. This exponentially increased the learning and communication around both projects. It also enhanced the understanding about how the same process improvement tool (such as a measurement plan, a process map, or a fishbone diagram) could be applied to two different processes with such different outcomes.

"One creative member of the team came up with the idea of calling our work area 'Kaizenville', which indicates that while the work was performed with the utmost seriousness, the teams also really enjoyed being immersed in the process of process improvement", says Blair.

"We also engaged in a process improvement project to facilitate our ability to estimate the cost of an activity. This was the first time we attempted to use the DMAIC methodology and the tools and Legal Lean Sigma to help us get a better handle on how we approached pricing, budgeting, and planning a project, as well as competitive assessment and improvement identification."

This estimating project team began by highlighting the issues around the eData group, which had a great deal of data, but not all the right information needed to understand what it meant, the variability in processes, and the way they are operated across the group. "Ultimately, we wound up possessing significantly greater abilities to quantify what factors *most* drive the cost of an activity and *how* they drive the cost", said Blair. "And, from a management perspective, it was critical to develop a methodology that can be applied to all or almost all key activities plus determine a way to update the estimates a couple of times a year to capture what we've learned. We want to be the best at this and that means we have to continuously improve."

Morgan Lewis's eData practice was just getting started, serving as a host firm for the Legal Lean Sigma Institute's open enrollment certification course in 2013, and also layering on project management skill development. In 2014, the eData group engaged the Legal Lean Sigma Institute to deliver another privately delivered Yellow Belt certification course. But this one was different. It was the first one that was specifically tailored to include clients.

At each table, a Morgan Lewis client and client team spent two days working together. Each team used a selected process for the duration of the certification course to use in their table work. This allowed them to both learn how to apply tools and concepts using a relevant example, and simultaneously to discuss areas where both the firm and the client could work together to improve the process.

Morgan Lewis's successful approach should serve as a model for how other law firms can develop skills and use the educational experience to learn and begin working with clients. As Blair puts it: "Inviting our clients to join us in our pursuit of continuous process improvement by training together on Lean Sigma has been a unique way to enhance already great relationships with key clients. Sharing a common process language and commitment to continuous process improvement aligns us with our clients in a way no other outreach can."

Using Lean Six Sigma to further client relationships
Eversheds
While this Morgan Lewis example provides one model approach, there certainly are other ways of using process improvement methodologies and Lean Six Sigma tools to further relationships with clients. One of the options is for the law firm to provide consulting services. For example, Eversheds has several consultancies and a couple of different staffing models to help the firm and its clients streamline procedures and control costs. One of the consultancies, Eversheds Consulting, was designed to help in-house legal teams address the challenges of running their departments efficiently, to use new technologies in order to facilitate process improvement, and to help the legal department provide better value to their businesses.

Clifford Chance

Clifford Chance used process improvement with clients in its banking practice: "Through our discussions with a key banking client, we became aware that a regular transaction we perform for them was taking longer than was ideal. We agreed with the client that improvements could be made and kicked off a joint Continuous Improvement project. An intensive two day workshop, attended by Clifford Chance partners and associates and three representatives from the client, analysed every step in the existing process, with the help of two of our Continuous Improvement specialists. The workshop identified the causes of delays and agreed changes to be made on both sides. Since implementing the changes, many of these transactions are completing up to 40% faster than before. Moreover, our two teams now understand each other better and are working together in a more joined up way."[9]

DuPont Legal

While some law firms are new to this, others have been immersed in process improvement with their clients for a significant amount of time. DuPont Legal has led the change in how legal departments partner with outside counsel. In a 2001 article, Thomas L. Sager, vice president and assistant general counsel at DuPont Legal and a Six Sigma Champion, and Scott L. Winkelman, a partner with the law firm Crowell & Moring LLP, engagement partner to DuPont, a Six Sigma Black Belt, and chair of the firm's eBusiness Group, shared their experiences:

"Everyone (both inside and outside) focuses on the right solution for the client, in this case DuPont. That focus may mean fewer resources allocated to a given task. But we all learn from the process and become more competitive in our respective marketplaces. This focus also explains, in part, why we chose two professionals from our outside network to join our Six Sigma effort and to become Black Belts... The fact that core features of Six Sigma – attention to efficiency, elimination of process defects and redundancies, and striving for process standardization – are countercultural for lawyers is merely one more reason to embrace Six Sigma, because attorneys often are most in need for the wake-up call that Six Sigma provides."[10]

Employing Lean and Six Sigma in in-house law departments

In the article,[11] Michelle Fujimoto of Shook Hardy & Bacon and Eric D. Brown of Eli Lilly & Company discuss the applicability of Lean and

Six Sigma methodologies and tools to legal work performed by both in-house departments and in law firms: "[I]n contrast to in-house lawyers who operate in a business environment and are directly influenced by business thinking and methodologies that are employed in their corporations, law firms are more likely to be skeptical about the applicability of data-and-predictability-driven management processes to the practice of law. Over the last few years, this difference in mindset and the strength of inertia have resulted in a gulf between how in-house lawyers and many outside counsel approach the business and the practice of law. Many would say that a culture shift is absolutely necessary for a law firm to thrive, perhaps even to survive, in the current competitive landscape that is increasingly driven by data, predictability, and cost control, in addition to the older currency of relationships and reputations."

Additionally, they report that "Shook Hardy & Bacon (Shook) partnered with a client to utilize Lean Six Sigma tools for a patent application process. The project focused on two goals: (1) to reduce the amount of time it takes to process an application from start to finish; and (2) to reduce the time from the date of assignment to the date the application is filed with the patent office. Shook worked with the client and used various tools, including process maps and cause-and-effect diagrams, to prepare a step-by-step analysis of the entire process. Tasks or functions were then identified for modification or elimination."

With so many client satisfaction studies demonstrating that it is critically important to understand a client's business and be their partner, using Lean and Six Sigma to identify and help clients solve priority problems and seize important opportunities is an excellent way to demonstrate understanding and a commitment to a business partnership. Furthermore, process improvement provides a framework for approaching and discussing business goals in ways that allow those delivering legal services to become more than a service provider and to perform more as a business partner with legal expertise.

This approach is in no way limited to law firms; in fact, it is being successfully employed by alternative providers who now compete for and perform work that used to be the bread and butter of law firms. The issue for some law firms that are not engaged in process improvement is that they do not have the same compelling culture and mindset of continuous improvement, or metrics around what it takes to do and deliver particular kinds of work, and so they are at a serious disadvantage when it comes to competing for the same clients with firms that are engaged in process improvement.

A powerful collaboration: Integreon and Microsoft

Integreon and Microsoft demonstrated the power of combining forces to develop contract review processes that deliver high quality – and faster – services at a lower cost. In October 2013, Integreon won the International Association for Contract and Commercial Management's 2013 Innovation Award for "Outstanding Service Provider" for its contract management services and support to Microsoft Corporation.

In an Integreon press release, Lucy Bassli, Microsoft's assistant general counsel, explained the background to the collaboration: "Four years ago we began the search for a service provider who could go beyond mere augmentation of resources and help us re-design and improve upon our contract review processes. Through the relationship we established with Integreon, we've seen a dramatic improvement in the efficiency of our contract review process. Our in-house team has also been able to focus on higher level activities while furthering their own legal careers here at Microsoft."[12]

The press release further explains that "prior to engaging with Integreon, Microsoft realized that its existing paralegal resourcing model for legal contract review was not sustainable in the long term. The volume of procurement contracts flowing into Microsoft's Global Contracting Office was significant and growing rapidly. The turnaround time for legal review was averaging three days per contract and causing delays in the procurement process for needed goods and services. In response, Microsoft initiated a dual track effort to study their current contract processes and the opportunities offered by legal process outsourcing (LPO). After a rigorous selection process, Microsoft selected Integreon as its LPO partner.

Integreon's paralegals and lawyers operating from delivery centers in Fargo, North Dakota and Bristol, UK work as an extension of the Microsoft legal department. The close collaboration and integration of the Integreon and Microsoft teams ensured that the engagement realized short-term successes and laid the groundwork for expansion of the program as greater volumes and types of contracts, including foreign language contracts, were brought into scope.

Microsoft's cost for legal contract review has been significantly reduced. Today, the Integreon teams in Fargo and Bristol handle 20,000 contracts per year in 14 languages and across 125 countries. At the same time, the average turnaround time for legal review has dropped from three days to less than one, and the percentage of contracts meeting the agreed-upon turnaround time has increased from 86 percent to

99 percent. The increased productivity and reduced costs to manage contracts were complemented by high quality output, as results consistently exceed Microsoft's 98.4 percent quality target.

"The success we've had at Microsoft and our recognition from the IACCM demonstrate that the traditional model for legal services delivery can be changed for the better. Integreon has the legal process re-engineering expertise, industry knowledge, and global delivery platform that allow us to provide our clients with substantial legal process improvement in tandem with cost reduction", said Brent Larlee, global head of Legal Services at Integreon. "Ours is not simply a cost arbitrage approach. It is about aligning the right resources with the right tasks to deliver the right outcomes while still reducing cost."

Thompson Hine: "Client needs – firm heeds"

Some firms, while talking the talk and making bold statements about their focus on "value" and being "client centered", still are not demonstrating that they are actively listening to what the clients say is valuable to them. After many years of corporate clients being extremely vocal about their needs, desires, and expectations, there are still plenty of opportunities to demonstrate that firms are listening and taking action. Some firms, on the other hand, are doing just this – and the number of those firms is on the rise.

For every firm that is not doing a good job with "voice of the client", there is a provider, or five, or 10, or 50 that is – and these providers are actively pursuing that firm's clients for business. It is only a matter of time before those clients turn elsewhere. No firm can afford to rest on its laurels or take any client for granted; this is why having a firm-wide culture of continuous improvement is so important.

Thompson Hine has a long history of aligning with the needs that clients say are most vital to them. The firm's published "Client Service Pledge" was a first in the industry, and remains one of the few in existence. Thompson Hine's managing partner, Deborah Read, leads by example with the philosophy "client needs – firm heeds". This cultural imperative has driven structure and purpose in the firm according to what is most valued by clients – and has continued to adapt that alignment over time as client needs change.

The BTI Consulting Group has tracked the changing goals of corporate counsel through their annual benchmarking survey. In their latest report surveying over 300 corporate counsel, it is noteworthy that corporate counsel list "delivering more value" as their top goal (for the second consecutive year) and "controlling legal costs" as the next most important goal.

Heeding this nuanced and important shift, Thomson Hine has undertaken more structure to fulfill that client need. The firm's considerable investment in legal project management (LPM) to drive greater predictability, cost management, client communication and, ultimately, value is an important component of their value-focus. This, combined with value-billing, broader thinking around how to efficiently and cost-effectively staff matters, and process improvements that are a natural outgrowth of LPM support their value focus. Ms Read notes: "These efforts must become a part of the fabric of the legal practice or we are simply not delivering the value promise to our clients. Experience and a brilliant legal mind are just not enough. We have to approach our work consistently in a way that brings the client and firm together at the outset of an engagement, aligning goals and work approach, understanding cost/benefit expectations, and efficiently completing the work in a manner that avoids surprises along the way."

Why have some firms waited for the clients to drive these changes? Why would any organization decide not to make things better until their collective back is up against a wall? Even if a firm is only driven by self-interest – which is something I have never observed, as the thousands of lawyers and business professionals I have worked with have all cared deeply about clients – the evidence is abundant that delivering better value to firm clients results in increased profitability.

The culture shift
It has now been five years since the ACC launched its Value Index, an online service for ACC members on which in-house counsel evaluate their law firms based on six performance criteria:

1. Understands objectives/expectations;

2. Legal expertise;

3. Efficiency/process management,

4. Responsiveness/communication,

5. Predictable cost/budgeting skills; and

6. Results delivered/execution.

The ACC's publication entitled "The ACC Value Index, Key Insights"[13] reports the top three things corporate counsel want in a law firm as:

1. Value;
2. Responsiveness/communication;
3. Legal expertise.

On the other hand, in-house counsel are "most dissatisfied" with:

1. Value;
2. Predictable cost/budgeting skills; and
3. Responsiveness/communication.

Jennifer J. Salopek's article on the nominees for ACC's 2014 Value Challenge notes an "evolution" that has occurred since the program was launched, just three years before: "Whereas value-based fee arrangements were front and center during the first year of our program, they are now part of a comprehensive approach that reflects a ground-level cultural change in the in-house practice of law. As legal departments align more closely with their customers and apply strategies and tactics common to the business units they serve, they are shifting their culture to one of greater transparency, solid partnerships and more sophisticated practice. The result has been a win-win: enhanced satisfaction among the lawyers and their clients."[14]

"It's gratifying to see law department leaders put leading-edge business tactics into practice to improve and demonstrate the value of the legal department", says Catherine J. Moynihan, ACC's senior director of Legal Management Services. "There was intense focus on value-based pricing when we launched the ACC Value Challenge. It's nice to see that it's become mainstream, just one part of comprehensive value programs that legal departments are implementing."

The thinking behind Lean Six Sigma and finding the lowest cost resource that is capable of doing each task in a process is evident in Salopek's report: "One common theme among this year's ACC Value Champions was a strategic approach to sourcing and staffing of legal matters. Whether you call them lanes, buckets, or chunks, these work divisions and assignments evidence a realization that one size of legal service does not fit all; and that decisions about the resources being used – internally and externally – must be made with value in mind. The catchphrase is 'disaggregation:' thinking about each kind of work and what resources might be deployed to match effort to value."

There are significant opportunities for law firms to anticipate and be much more proactive in discussing and understanding the opportunities to address client needs. By employing Lean Six Sigma thinking and frameworks, they can do so continuously and in collaboration with their clients. Lean Six Sigma provides the framework and tools to transform the conversations that law firms and clients are having about how they do and deliver their work – together. As such, Lean Six Sigma not only improves processes, it enhances the relationships of the people that the processes are serving.

References

1. White, J., "Cost Control is Not the Final Answer", 28 March 2014; see http://legalvaluetheory.com/2014/03/28/cost-control-is-not-the-final-answer.

2. Ibid.

3. iSixSigma, "Six Sigma Saves a Fortune", *iSixSigma* magazine, January/February 2007.

4. ALM Legal Intelligence, "Pricing Professionals – Essential to Law Firms, An Ally to Clients" (white paper), 2014.

5. Duncan, S. S., "5 Firms Take Bold Approaches", ABA *Law Practice* magazine, volume 38, No. 6, November/December 2012; see www.americanbar.org/publications/law_practice_magazine/2012/november-december/5-firms-take-bold-approaches.html.

6. Duncan, S. S., "The Progressive Model for Law Firm/Client Partnering", ABA *Law Practice* magazine, vol. 38, No. 6, November/December 2012.

7. In another related article, "8 Tips for Innovative Client Service", ABA *Law Practice* Magazine, vol. 38, No. 6, November/December 2012; see www.americanbar.org/publications/law_practice_magazine/2012/november-december/8-tips-for-innovative-client-service.html.

8. Davis, D. "Lawyers jump into process improvement", 28 March 2014, *Process Excellent Network*; see www.processexcellencenetwork.com/lean-six-sigma-business-transformation/articles/lawyers-jump-into-process-improvement.

9. Clifford Chance, "Applying Continuous Improvement to high-end legal services"; whitepaper available at www.cliffordchance.com/content/dam/cliffordchance/About_us/Continuous_Improvement_White_Paper.pdf.

10. Sager, T.L., and Winkelman, S.L., "Six Sigma: Positioning for Competitive Advantage", ACCA Docket 19, no. 1, 2001.

11. Fujimoto, M., and Brown, E.D., "Lean Six Sigma: What You Don't Know Can Hurt You".

12. Ibid. http://www.integreon.com/blog/2013/10/integreon-wins-iaccm-2013-innovation-award-for-outstanding-contract-management-services-and-support-to-microsoft-corporation.html

13. Association of Corporate Council, "The ACC Value Index: Key Insights",

14. Salopek, J. J., "Meet The 2014 ACC Value Champions, Transforming The Corporate Legal Function To Drive Value", Association of Corporate Counsel online; see www.acc.com/valuechallenge/valuechamps/2014introduction.cfm.